SWITZERLAND

ALSO BY PAUL HOFMANN

*The Spell of the Vienna Woods: Inspiration and
Influence from Beethoven to Kafka*

Roma: The Smart Traveler's Guide to the Eternal City

That Fine Italian Hand

Cento Città

The Viennese

O Vatican! A Slightly Wicked View of the Holy See

Rome: The Sweet, Tempestuous Life

SWITZERLAND

The Smart Traveler's Guide to Zurich, Basel, and Geneva

PAUL HOFMANN

HENRY HOLT AND COMPANY
New York

Henry Holt and Company, Inc.
Publishers since 1866
115 West 18th Street
New York, New York 10011

Henry Holt® is a registered
trademark of Henry Holt and Company, Inc.

Published in Canada by Fitzhenry & Whiteside Ltd.,
195 Allstate Parkway, Markham, Ontario L3R 4T8.

Library of Congress Cataloging-in-Publication Data
Hofmann, Paul.
Switzerland : the smart traveler's guide to Zurich, Basel, and
Geneva / Paul Hofmann.—1st ed.
p. cm.
Includes index.
1. Switzerland—Guidebooks. 2. Zurich (Switzerland)—Guidebooks.
3. Basel (Switzerland)—Guidebooks. 4. Geneva (Switzerland)—
Guidebooks. I. Title.
DQ16.H64 1994   93-7756
914.9404'73—dc20   CIP

ISBN 0-8050-2596-0
ISBN 0-8050-3588-5 (An Owl Book: pbk.)

Henry Holt books are available for special promotions and
premiums. For details contact: Director, Special Markets.

First published in hardcover in 1994 by
Henry Holt and Company, Inc.

First Owl Book Edition—1995

Designed by Katy Riegel
Maps by Jeffrey L. Ward

Printed in the United States of America
All first editions are printed on acid-free paper.∞

1 3 5 7 9 10 8 6 4 2
1 3 5 7 9 10 8 6 4 2
(pbk.)

Contents

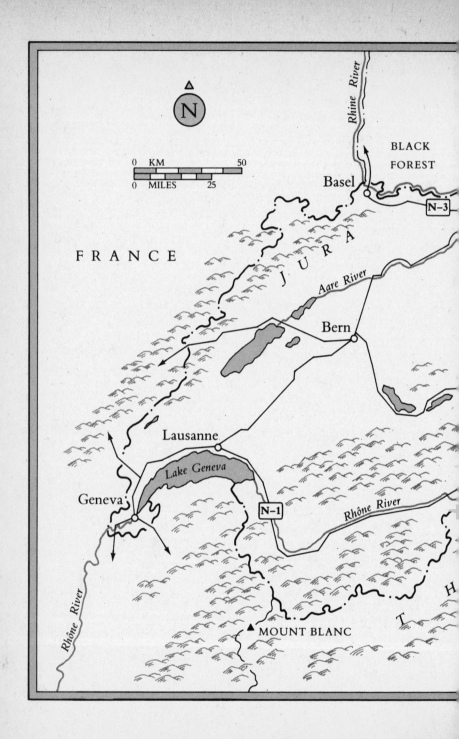

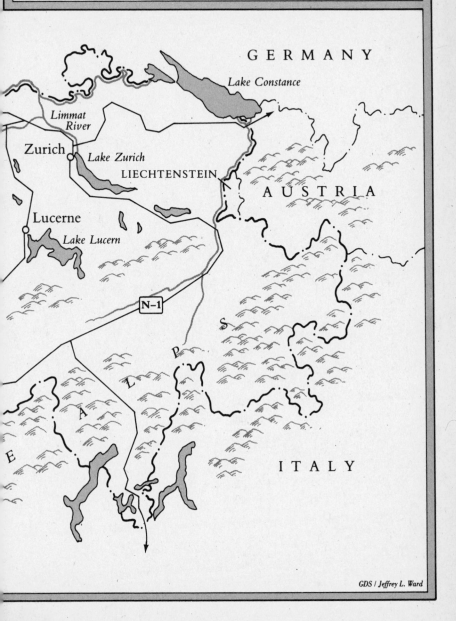

SWITZERLAND

GERMANY

Lake Constance

Limmat
River

Zurich

Lake Zurich

LIECHTENSTEIN

AUSTRIA

Lucerne

Lake Lucern

N–1

A L P S

E A L

ITALY

GDS / Jeffrey L. Ward

1.

A Rich Trio

ZURICH, BASEL, AND GENEVA each have distinctive characteristics—hardly surprising in a nation that has long thrived on diversity. On a territory that is only one-third the area of New York State, situated in the Alpine heart of the Continent, Switzerland accommodates people speaking four languages and many dialects, three major religions, and twenty-six cantons and half cantons—each a semiautonomous republic with its own legislature, government, judiciary, and police. The Canton of Geneva and the Half Canton of Basel-Stadt are almost completely taken up by either city and its suburbs. The relatively large and densely populated Canton of Zurich is made up of other cities and towns in addition to the country's largest metropolitan conglomeration.

None of the three biggest cities is the capital of Switzerland. This is old, picturesque Bern (population 140,000) near the geographical center of the confederation, 80 miles (125 kilometers) distant from Zurich, 60 miles (95 kilometers) from Basel, and 97 miles (154 kilometers) from Geneva. The federal Parliament and Government have their

seats in Bern; the country's supreme judiciary body, the
Federal Court, sits in Lausanne.

Zurich and Geneva are important gateways of intercontinental air traffic; Basel, on a sharp bend of the Rhine, is
a river port representing the landlocked country's sole out-
let to the high seas. Mountains are always close in Switzerland. The soaring Mont Blanc massif, with Europe's
highest peak, is visible from Geneva; other Alpine ranges
can be seen from Zurich; and from Basel it's not far to the
forested slopes of the Jura. Zurich functions as an international financial center in close contact with Wall Street,
London, Tokyo, and Hong Kong. Basel is the seat of
the Bank for International Settlements—a monetary world
clearinghouse—and of multinational corporations that are
leaders in the chemical and pharmaceutical fields. Geneva,
with a vast United Nations complex and the headquarters
of many global agencies, is Europe's most cosmopolitan
metropolis.

All three cities are prime trading posts of the international art market with periodic auctions and hundreds of
private galleries. Zurich, Basel, and Geneva display treasures from all civilizations and continents in their well-
ordered museums. They boast an intense musical and
theatrical life and are proud of their institutions of higher
learning and advanced research; their vaunted clinics attract
patients from faraway nations.

Travelers visiting Zurich, Basel, or Geneva, or all three
of them, can count on reliable communications, satisfactory hotels (some of them ranked among the world's best),
fine restaurants, clean and generally safe streets, stores with
merchandise from all over the world, and a general sense
of efficiency.

Prices for most items and services will seem high. Switzerland is, after all, one of the richest countries on earth

with an enviably high standard of living and with a large portion of citizens who, whenever they do spend money, want the best. Yet guests of hotels and eating places as well as shoppers will be pleased to find they get value for what they pay.

The courtesy that foreigners encounter in hotels, restaurants, and stores will often appear impersonal, and they will sense an underlying reserve in the Swiss people with whom they happen to be dealing. Smiles don't come easily to Swiss faces. Consciously or unconsciously, many Swiss distrust outsiders and newcomers. Moneyed visitors are of course always welcome in a country that for centuries has derived a good part of its income from banking and the tourist industry. This does not mean that the local people expect every traveler who is coming through to spend liberally. If you look and act like someone who is well off, you will gain, not lose, respect in Switzerland when you painstakingly inquire about room rates in hotels or prices in restaurants and shops: you prove thereby that, just like your hosts, you give sober consideration to the value of money.

Besides an ingrained sense of thrift in a confederation whose founding fathers were hardscrabble mountain farmers, the traditional virtues and values of the Swiss are tenacity, trustworthiness, and an all-pervasive love of order and neatness. Pedestrians in the cities will patiently wait for the green light at crosswalks even when no oncoming traffic is visible. If you jaywalk or drop a candy wrapper on the sidewalk, you may draw stern looks or even a censorious mutter from bystanders. Given the national character, it's best to avoid being late for an appointment with a Swiss.

Critics of the Swiss have often charged them with smugness and a lack of grace to the point of stodginess. One of the stereotypes about the Swiss is that they don't have a sense of humor; yet the week-long madness of carnival time in Basel (p. 133), believed to be Switzerland's wealthiest city, belies the cliché of the dull Swiss.

It is not without a certain self-irony—especially among young people—that urban populations at various times every year revive the traditions of their folklore: all those medieval costumes and quaint parades. The three major Swiss cities have histories that go back far before the foundation of the Helvetian Confederation in A.D. 1291. Zurich, Basel, and Geneva were originally ancient Roman settlements and had a vigorous civic life in the Middle Ages. Today they lovingly maintain their old buildings and neighborhoods and are proud of their traditions.

The first impression the visitor gets is nevertheless one of modernness and no-nonsense efficiency. Despite this widespread well-being, none of the three cities is spared present-day urban ills. Zurich in particular has a serious drug problem, and the incidence of AIDS in Switzerland in relation to the number of residents is among Europe's highest. Street crime in the three cities, often related to narcotics addiction or alcoholism, is on the increase, although muggings, robberies, assaults, and thefts are still rare in comparison with other Western centers.

SWISS DIVERSITY AND LANGUAGES

The official language of Zurich and Basel is German, but in everyday life people of either city use their local patois, belonging to the group of the Alemannic dialects of German as spoken also in the Alsace, southwest Germany, and western Austria. Natives of Zurich and Basel are thus at least bilingual: They learn standard German, which they call the *Schriftsprache* or *Hochdeutsch* (written language of high German) in school, read it in books and newspapers, and hear it sometimes on television and radio. When they speak what they think is standard German, they still use Swiss particularities, like *merci* (the French word, but stressed on the first syllable) for *danke* (thank you). Among themselves, or with other Alemannic Swiss, the Zurichers and Baselers communicate in their local brands of *Schwyzerdütsch* (Swiss German), or dialect; the Zurich variety is different from the Basel idiom. Even if you are fluent in German, you won't easily understand Zurichers or Baselers talking the way they are used to or one of the frequent broadcasts in *Schwyzerdütsch*. Addressed in standard German, an Alemannic Swiss will readily switch to *Schriftsprache*, but never, never call a German-speaking Swiss a German!

The French spoken by natives of Geneva is hardly different from normal talk in France's adjoining Savoy region and the nearby city of Lyon, although it is recognizably different in accent and tempo from Parisian French. There are only a few oddities in the Geneva-French vocabulary (p. 150).

German, French, Italian, and Romansh—an ancient idiom spoken by some fifty thousand persons in the southeastern Canton of Grisons—are Switzerland's national languages. Many citizens know at least two of the four tongues, although more German-speaking Swiss are also familiar with French than the other way around.

English has lately become Switzerland's unofficial fifth (or second) language, especially in the three major cities; it seems well on its way to developing into a vehicle of communication between the various linguistic groups. At the prestigious Federal Polytechnic College in Zurich, for instance, teachers and students from different parts of

Switzerland often fall back on English, and many public announcements and directional signs are also in that language. A foreign visitor to Zurich, Basel, or Geneva will have little difficulty finding someone who understands and speaks English.

Foreigners are conspicuous in Zurich and Basel, and especially in Geneva, as they are to varying degrees all over Switzerland. At least 16 percent of the country's resident population—more than a million persons—lack Swiss citizenship, although they may have picked up the local dialect. (Some Alemannic cantons demand that candidates for naturalization speak or at least understand *Schwyzerdütsch*.) In Geneva, which is virtually surrounded by France, and in Basel, on whose outskirts the borders of Switzerland, France, and Germany converge, thousands of foreign commuters—the *frontaliers*—cross the frontiers every working day on their way to and from jobs in either city. Hotel and restaurant staffs in Zurich, Basel, and Geneva, as elsewhere in the country, include many Portuguese, Spaniards, Italians, Greeks, Turks, and people from what used to be Yugoslavia. Geneva, in particular, lately experienced also a sizable influx of North Africans.

THE EVERLASTING LEAGUE

Prehistoric settlers lived on or near the sites of the three biggest Swiss cities and built dwellings on piles off the shores of the lakes of Zurich and Geneva. In the first century B.C. the three areas were inhabited by a Celtic people whom the Romans called Helvetians when they conquered and colonized what is today Switzerland. Zurich derives its name from an ancient Roman customs station; the impressive ruins of a town that flourished under Emperor

Augustus is a sightseeing spot near Basel; and Geneva was a prosperous trade center of the Roman Empire.

After the barbarian invasions and the Dark Ages, Zurich, Basel, and Geneva developed into commercial centers with a well-to-do class of burghers. Their cathedrals date from the High Middle Ages, and the surviving medieval and Renaissance houses in their oldest neighborhoods attest to early prosperity. The three cities brought forth their own scholars and artists and attracted others from abroad; the new art of book printing soon flourished, especially in Basel. Great religious reformers—Calvin in Geneva and Zwingli in Zurich—became internationally influential.

Switzerland's three principal cities are today predominantly Protestant, but the Roman Catholic Church is conspicuously represented, and Jewish communities are well established. The first international Zionist Congress was held in Basel in 1897. Geneva, more than the two other big Swiss cities, has lately experienced an immigration of Muslims, mainly from North Africa.

In 1351 Zurich joined the Everlasting League, an alliance that the Forest Cantons of Uri, Schwyz, and Unterwalden had concluded in 1291—the nucleus of Switzerland. Basel was admitted into the confederation in 1501, Geneva only in 1815. (Today, Switzerland identifies itself on coins and in other official contexts as Confoederatio Helvetica [Latin for Helvetian Confederation]; the *CH* in the international motor vehicle registration code for Switzerland is an abbreviation of its Latin name.) The confederation grew from a league of mountaineers to repel encroachments by an aristocratic family, the Habsburgs, who had their origins in the east of what is today Switzerland and were to become the rulers of Austria and a vast empire. Since their medieval resistance to would-be overlords, the Swiss struggled through the centuries, with varying degrees of success, against interference by outsiders. Napoleon's troops occupied Switzerland, and after his fall the European powers in the Congress of Vienna in 1815 proclaimed the perpetual neutrality of the confederation.

The visitor to Zurich, Basel, or Geneva may therefore be puzzled to see groups of Swiss soldiers with complete field gear in the railroad terminals, especially on weekends. At times it looks as if the neutral country were mobilizing its army as soldiers carrying automatic weapons, steel helmets fastened to their heavy backpacks, gas masks at the ready, pile into trains. The fact is that every able-bodied Swiss man between the ages of twenty and fifty is periodically recalled to his army unit for military exercises or refresher courses of two or three weeks until he has served at least 330 days on active duty after basic training. Under the Swiss military system every citizen-soldier keeps his firearm at home and is responsible for its maintenance. If you look for a Swiss banker or businessman whose name has been given to you as a possible contact, his office may tell you that he happens to be on duty with his battalion and will be back in a week or two. Army officers who in civilian life hold executive positions in local government or in private enterprise form an unofficial network that is essential to the way Switzerland functions.

It is often said that Switzerland doesn't have an army but rather *is* an army. What this neutral country with a population of 6.6 million does have is a very small cadre of professional military men and a thoroughly trained militia. In case of an emergency, Switzerland could mobilize a formidable force of more than 600,000 men within days. A few thousand women volunteers are assigned noncombatant military tasks.

Even Hitler, faced with the prospect of tough resistance in the mountainous country, refrained from invading it.

Although the dangers of an attack on Switzerland or of serious skirmishes on its borders have lately receded, the Swiss keep doggedly preparing themselves for the worst. (In a referendum in 1989, however, no fewer than 35.6 percent of all voters demanded complete abolition of the Swiss army.)

TRANSPORTATION AND COMMUNICATIONS

Many thousands hasten through the rail stations of Zurich, Basel, and Geneva at the beginning and end of every working day on their way to and from their city jobs. Commuting from suburbs and more distant towns is made comparatively easy by **railroad services** that are justly renowned. The three major cities are linked with one another by frequent, fast trains. Between Zurich and Basel, trains run at half-hour intervals from early morning to late at night, taking about an hour for the trip. Between Zurich and Geneva there is at least one train every hour from 6 A.M. to 10 P.M., with about three hours' travel time. Trains between Geneva and Basel run at hourly intervals, the trip lasting from two hours and forty minutes to three hours.

Motorways and a network of good **highways** connect the three principal cities. The distances are: Zurich to Basel, 53 miles (85 kilometers); Zurich to Geneva, 174 miles (278 kilometers); and Basel to Geneva, 156 miles (249 kilometers). Curbside parking and parking lots are limited at the centers of the three cities, and the parking garages in their downtown sections fill up early on working days.

All three main cities control important **waterways.** Geneva lies at the western end of the largest Alpine lake; Zurich hugs the bay where the Limmat River flows out of another big lake; and oceangoing boats sail from the North Sea up the Rhine to Basel.

The municipal **mass transit** networks of Zurich, Basel, and Geneva operate mainly tramcars and buses; lake boats are also part of the public transportation systems in Zurich and Geneva. Bicycles can be rented for about $10 a day at every station of the Swiss Federal Railways.

Cabs are plentiful in all three cities and can be summoned by phone via radio-dispatch services. Taxi rates are higher than in U.S. cities, drivers expecting a tip of 5 to 10 percent of the fare.

Swiss **telephone service** is exemplary. If you have enough coins, you can reach almost any number around the globe by dialing it directly from any pay phone. For operator assistance, call 114. Hotels are authorized to collect substantial service charges in addition to the official telephone tolls for calls made from their premises (except from pay phones). Hotel guests are advised to place overseas calls and, if they want to save money, as many other calls as they can from post offices.

The central **post offices** in Zurich, Basel, and Geneva and other major post offices (generally marked PTT), especially at the railroad terminals and airports, have telephone sections with a large number of individual booths. Enter any free booth, place your calls, and afterward pay for them at the desk. You will get a receipt recording the numbers you called, the length of the calls, the date and hour, and the charges. You may have to wait in line for a booth during afternoon and evening hours and on weekends. At these times the telephone sections, especially in the railroad terminals, tend to be crowded with non-Swiss "guest workers" and other immigrants who are calling relatives in Sri Lanka, Morocco, or some other distant country.

Some pay telephones can be used with prepaid cards

(Taxcard) as well as with coins. The cards can be bought at PTT offices and from many news vendors. The international country code for Switzerland is 43. The area code for Zurich is 01; for Basel, 061; for Geneva, 022.

Fax service is available at major PTT offices, hotels, and private storefront businesses.

Following is the Swiss spelling code for telephoning.

	GERMAN	FRENCH
A	Anna	Anna
B	Bertha	Berthe
C	Cäsar	Cécile
D	Daniel	Daniel
E	Emil	Emile
F	Friedrich	François
G	Gustav	Gustave
H	Heinrich	Henri
I	Ida	Ida
J	Jakob	Jeanne
K	Kaiser	Kilo
L	Leopold	Louise
M	Marie	Marie
N	Niklaus	Nicolas
O	Otto	Olga
P	Peter	Paul
Q	Quelle	Quittance
R	Rosa	Robert
S	Sophie	Suzanne
T	Theodor	Thérèse
U	Ulrich	Ulysse
V	Viktor	Victor
W	Wilhelm	William
X	Xaver	Xavier

| Y | Yverdon | Yvonne |
| Z | Zürich | Zurich |

HOTELS

Some of Europe's best hotels are to be found in Zurich, Basel, and Geneva, and standards even in simple establishments are acceptable.

Almost all houses in the three major cities, as in the rest of the country, are represented and classified by the Swiss Hotel Association, 130 Monbijoustrasse, 3001 Bern (031-507111, fax 031-507444). The association publishes each year a *Swiss Hotel Guide* listing establishments in all parts of the confederation, with their special characteristics and their room rates. Many travel agents keep the *Swiss Hotel Guide* available for consultation. Its text is in English in addition to German, French, and Italian. The *Swiss Hotel Guide* can be ordered from the Swiss Hotel Association in Bern or from any branch of the Swiss National Tourist Office, for instance: Swiss Center, 608 Fifth Avenue, New York, NY 10020 (212-757-5944); 150 North Michigan Avenue, Chicago, IL 60601 (312-630-5840); 222 N. Sepulveda Blvd., Los Angeles, CA 90245 (310-335-5980); 260 Stockton Street, San Francisco, CA 94108-5387 (415-362-2260); 154 University Avenue Toronto, Ont. M5H 3Y9 Canada (416-971-9734). In addition, the tourist information offices of Zurich, Basel, and Geneva (see their addresses and telephone and fax numbers in the sections devoted to each of the three cities) issue folders with the listings from the official *Swiss Hotel Guide* that pertain to their territory. These folders are freely available for the asking.

Swiss hotels are ranked according to the following categories: five stars, luxury class; four stars, first class; three stars, good middle class; two stars, comfortable; one star, plain. The official classification considers a number of criteria such as the number of staff in relation to the number of rooms, the amenities available to guests, and the standards of sanitary facilities.

The quality of breakfast and other hotel food is not considered in the official classification. Breakfast is generally, but not always, included in room rates. Many hotels offer self-service buffets in their breakfast rooms and sometimes charge extra for breakfast served in guest rooms. Hotels where only breakfast but no restaurant service is available are known as *hotels garnis*.

MONEY AND BANKS

The national currency is the Swiss franc. After a long period of monetary stability, its purchasing power has lately eroded as a result of moderate inflation, yet it still ranks among the world's hard and coveted monies.

Swiss bank notes come in denominations of 10 francs (orange), 20 francs (blue), 50 francs (green), 100 francs (blue), 500 francs (reddish brown) and 1,000 francs (violet). The following coins are in circulation: 5 Rappen (French: centimes); 10 and 20 Rappen/centimes; half-franc (50 Rappen/centimes); 1 franc; 2 francs; and 5 francs. Take care not to mix up the half-franc and 10 Rappen/centimes; they are almost identical in size and in metal-gray color, but the half-franc coin contains silver.

There are no restrictions on the import or export of Swiss and foreign money. Foreign bank notes can be sold or bought at any of the many banks at the day's official exchange rates, which are posted. Most banks pay a

slightly higher rate if you change a sizable amount in foreign currency (say, more than $2,000), but you will have
to ask for the additional point or two.

Centrally located bank branches in the major cities stay
open from 8 or 8:15 A.M. or even earlier to at least 4:30
P.M. Monday to Friday. Money exchanges at the airports
and railroad terminals have longer hours of operation and
also do business on Saturday and Sunday. Most bank
branches in central neighborhoods have automatic teller
machines that can be operated around the clock. The Euro-
check Card is the preferred bank card.

Many Swiss banks will open accounts for nonresident
foreigners who apply in person, submit proof of identity,
furnish a mailing address, and satisfy management that the
funds they want to deposit are of legal origin. On demand,
some banks provide substantial clients with so-called num-
bered accounts, marked only by a code (a group of figures
and maybe also letters). The identity of the account's
owner will be known only to a few executives of the bank
who are punishable under the law if they disclose it to
nonauthorized persons.

Swiss bank secrecy—often discussed inside and outside
the country—is by no means absolute. Swiss banks are
obliged to furnish information on their clients and their
assets to judiciary authorities (also non-Swiss ones) in
criminal investigations. Tax fraud committed in a foreign
country is regarded as a crime in Switzerland as well, but
tax evasion abroad that does not involve gross deception
will not fall under the Swiss definition of criminal tax
fraud. At any rate, the hundreds of big and small banks
listed in the telephone directories of Zurich, Basel, and
Geneva manage many billions of dollars' worth of foreign-
owned funds.

It is legal for U.S. citizens and residents to maintain

accounts at banks in Switzerland, but they may have to report on them to the U.S. Treasury Department by the appropriate Form TD F 90-22.1, as well as to the Internal Revenue Service.

EATING OUT

For restaurants, local culinary specialties, regional wines, and other beverages, see the appropriate sections under Zurich, Basel, and Geneva.

Helpings in Swiss eating places are usually very generous. Swiss wines, generally of satisfactory quality, are relatively expensive as compared with those available in nearby France and Italy. In restaurants, wines are often ordered in an open carafe by the deciliter—one, two, three, or five deciliters. A deciliter is 6.1 cubic inches or about the fifth part of a pint, filling a small wine glass.

Instead of wine, many restaurant patrons ask for beer, mineral water, or fruit juices. Coffee is generally of good quality; many restaurants serve Italian-type espresso and cappuccino on demand. Swiss chocolates are internationally renowned.

If you want food for snacks, picnics, or kitchenette cooking, you will find large selections in the many stores of the COOP chain, the MIGROS cooperatives, and other supermarkets, as well as in the food sections of the department stores. The sign *Aktion* (action) signals a special sale. Customers will be struck by the impressive arrays of cheeses and other dairy products. Fruits, often imported, are relatively expensive.

TIPPING

Service charges are included in all hotel bills and restaurant checks. At hotels the valet who parks your car and the bellman who carries your baggage up to your room will expect a moderate tip (2 to 5 francs). Tip the concierge who does you a special favor, getting you a flight ticket or a seat at the opera, for example. Tip the chambermaid if she pressed your clothes or rendered some other special service in addition to making up your room. In restaurants or cafés don't overtip but leave the small change on the plate, thus rounding off the amount on the check. As noted earlier, the tip for cabdrivers is 5 to 10 percent of the fare.

SHOPPING

Stores in the three major cities generally open at 8 or 9 A.M. Monday to Saturday and close at 6:30 P.M. Monday to Friday, at 4 P.M. Saturday. Many stores stay open until 9 P.M. on Thursday. Stores are closed on Sunday, some also on Monday morning.

Shops and offices remain closed on January 1 (in Zurich also on January 2), Good Friday, Easter Monday, Ascension Day (the Thursday forty days after Easter), Whitmonday (the Monday after Pentecost), August 1 (the Swiss national holiday, though many businesses close only in the afternoon), and December 25 and 26. Zurich, Basel, and Geneva also observe local holidays (pp. 82, 133, 197).

Foremost among the items to buy in Switzerland are its fine watches; they come in dazzling variety, from diamond-studded timepieces by prestigious firms to ever-new series of the best-selling plastic-encased Swatch numbers. Internationally popular as a souvenir and a useful all-purpose tool is the more than one-hundred-year-old Swiss Army Knife. The multiblade red knife with Switzerland's white cross is available in many different versions in countless gift and hardware shops. Other good buys in Switzerland: sportswear; chocolates; cheeses; woolen, cotton, and linen goods; hosiery; lace and embroideries; shoes; and art books.

2.

Zurich

ZURICH

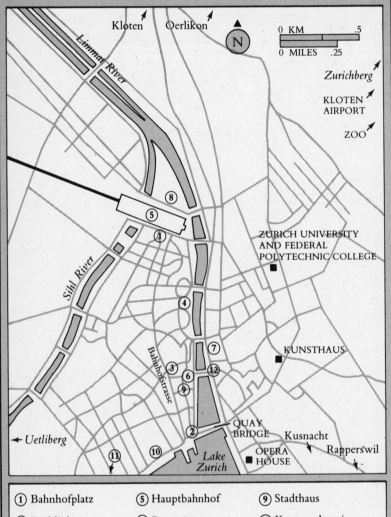

Kloten   Oerlikon

N

0 KM   .5
0 MILES   .25

Zurichberg

KLOTEN
AIRPORT

ZOO

Limmat River

Sihl River

⑧

⑤

①

ZURICH UNIVERSITY
AND FEDERAL
POLYTECHNIC COLLEGE

④

⑦

KUNSTHAUS

③ ⑥ ⑫
⑨

Bahnhofstrasse

②   QUAY
BRIDGE   Kusnacht

◄ *Uetliberg*

⑪   ⑩   Lake
Zurich   OPERA
HOUSE   Rapperswil

① Bahnhofplatz	⑤ Hauptbahnhof	⑨ Stadthaus
② Bürkliplatz	⑥ Fraumünster	⑩ Kongresshaus/ Tonhalle
③ Paradeplatz	⑦ Grossmünster	⑪ Rietberg Museum
④ Lindenhof	⑧ Swiss National Museum	⑫ Münster Bridge

SWITZERLAND'S BIGGEST CITY, 1,341 feet (409 meters) above sea level, is situated at the northern end of the elongated, curving Lake of Zurich. It occupies a vast area around the bay where the Limmat River leaves the lake to receive, a mile (1.6 kilometers) downstream, the Sihl River and to proceed to join the Aare, a tributary of the Rhine. The geographical lake-river system destined the place as a center of transportation and trade since prehistoric times.

The railroad builders of the nineteenth century ringed Zurich with strands of tracks, making it an important hub for passengers and freight. In the twentieth century the city emerged as a major gateway of intercontinental aviation at the convergence of a network of trans-European motor roads.

Zurich is framed by wooded hills—the Zürichberg to the east and the Uetliberg to the west. The Lake of Zurich reaches into the city center. This body of water, steadily renewed by fresh streams from Alpine glaciers and snowy ridges, is a remnant of the Ice Age; it is 25 miles (40 kilometers) long, 1.25 to 2.5 miles (2 to 4 kilometers) wide, and up to 469 feet (143 meters) deep, and it turns from Zurich toward the southeast.

Zurichers put a premium on living in a house or apartment with a lake view, especially a villa in one of the affluent suburbs on the eastern shore (the city's "Gold Coast"), and on owning a boat docked in a hard-to-get slot in one of the expensive marinas. In summer the bathing beaches on either lakeshore are crowded. Water treatment plants have kept lake pollution within acceptable limits.

The climate of Zurich is moderately continental. Winter temperatures are often below the freezing point, with occasional snowstorms; at the height of summer the heat rarely exceeds 86 degrees Fahrenheit (30 centigrade). A recurrent visitor to Zurich, especially in winter and spring, is a warm, dry wind from the south, called the *Föhn*. Whenever the squally *Föhn* blows, faraway mountains seem close, the air appears to assume a glassy quality, and some individuals experience a feeling of oppression and discomfort. During the winter months the sky over Zurich will be covered with gray clouds for weeks.

The residential population of Zurich is about 360,000; the metropolitan area, including a number of officially separate towns that virtually have become suburbs, is inhabited by at least another 500,000 people, many of whom commute to city jobs. Zurich is the capital of the Canton of Zurich, which comprises 171 municipalities in an area almost double that of New York City, with 1.1 million residents. To its natives the city is, in their patois, Züri (with the stress on the *ü*).

ARRIVAL AND DEPARTURE

Zurich's airport is in a plain near the industrial town of Kloten not quite 7 miles (11 kilometers) northeast of the city center. **Kloten Airport,** officially Flughafen Zürich, is among Europe's ten busiest civil aviation facilities, handling twelve million passengers annually. Its safety and security record is excellent. Terminal A handles all flights of Swissair, Scandinavian Airlines System (SAS), and Austrian Airlines (which are operating under a pool agreement), whereas Terminal B is reserved for other scheduled and charter services. The two terminals interconnect by walkways and people movers.

Passport controls are fast. Americans and citizens of most other Western countries need a valid passport but no visa for entry into Switzerland and for an uninterrupted stay in the country as tourists or visitors for up to three months.

Checked baggage is delivered speedily, and most arriving passengers are able to walk out of the terminal without having to submit to customs controls by following the green channel for travelers who have nothing to declare.

Personal belongings such as clothing, sports gear, toiletries, musical instruments, and amateur cameras may be imported duty free. A reasonable amount of food, such as a person would consume in a day, may also be brought in free. The Swiss customs regulations allow free importation of 2 liters (about 2 quarts) of alcoholic beverages per adult person as well as 400 cigarettes (200 cigarettes if the traveler is arriving from a European country). Souvenirs purchased in some other country and destined to be taken out again should be declared as transit goods to the Swiss customs officers on arrival.

Baggage carts are plentiful and free throughout the

airport complex and the adjoining rail station; they are "smart carts" that can also be used on the escalators. Passengers will find banks, PTT offices, tourist and hotel information bureaus, a pharmacy, nurseries, restaurants, and newsstands as well as other services and businesses at both terminals. Wheelchairs can be obtained free of charge for use in the airport, and there is ample space for them in the elevators. Car rental firms are located on the fifth level of Parking Garage B (Parkhaus B), which can be reached from Terminal B by escalator, elevator, or stairs.

Check-in of departing passengers is usually speedy. After moving through passport control, travelers find a large duty-free shop and other stores and boutiques in the departure lounge.

Some Kloten Airport telephone numbers: flight information, 8127111; airport management, 8162211; police, 8140050; customs, 8162051.

Kloten Airport is linked with Zurich's main railroad terminal (Hauptbahnhof; see below) by trains departing or arriving at an underground station in front of Terminal B at intervals of ten to twenty minutes. Buy tickets at the windows of the ticket office or from a vending machine. The one-way fare is around $3 in second class and $5 in first class. The trip from the airport to Hauptbahnhof or vice versa, sometimes with a brief stop at the suburban station of Oerlikon, takes about ten minutes. Many of the trains connecting the airport with the Zurich rail terminal come from, or proceed to, such cities as Winterthur, St. Gall, or Bern. Arriving air passengers usually find ample space for themselves and their baggage in second-class coaches except during the weekday morning rush period (7 to 8 A.M.) when trains arriving at the airport station from Winterthur or St. Gall tend to be crowded with commuters. For a more comfortable train ride at that time, buy a first-class ticket.

A cab ride from Kloten Airport to downtown Zurich costs around $30. Many hotels provide limousine or minibus service for patrons. Taxis and buses stop in front of Terminal B.

Zurich's main railroad terminal **(Hauptbahnhof)** opened in 1871 and at present handles some five hundred trains a day. (Switchboard, 2453111; information, 2115010.) More than 100,000 persons pass through the sprawling structure every twenty-four hours. Fast EuroCity trains and night express trains with sleepers arrive from Paris, Milan, Rome, Vienna, Munich, and other centers on the Continent or depart from Hauptbahnhof for these destinations; quite a number of trains are in transit, stopping at the Zurich terminal for ten or fifteen minutes and pulling out again.

Since the late 1970s the Hauptbahnhof complex has been rebuilt and expanded in a vast project scheduled to be completed by the year 2000. The eclectic beaux arts architecture of the facade and the original large concourse are preserved as monuments to the great railroad age of the nineteenth century.

During the 1980s Zurich's engineers and architects built a modern terminal on three subterranean levels below the old station, for the city's Schnellbahn (Fast Railroad), a commuter system linking the center with many suburbs (see next section).

Underneath the Bahnhofplatz (Station Square) in front of the terminal is a shopping mall, known as Shopville. More shopping arcades were added on lower levels when the Schnellbahn platforms were created. Also on underground levels are rows of self-service lockers, a telephone office with many booths, and public toilets. There is also a "ticketeria" where tickets for the regional mass transit network are sold and information can be obtained.

Federal Railways ticket and information offices are on the street floor of Hauptbahnhof. On the same main level are the city's Tourist Information Office (Verkehrsverein, telephone 2114000), a Swissair office, a post office, a money exchange, various restaurants, and refreshment stands. The phone number for the lost property office (Fundbüro) at the terminal is 2118811; for the police station, 2472211.

Motorists arriving from Geneva, Bern, St. Gall, or Constance on Motor Road N-1, Switzerland's principal east-west road axis, or from Basel, Paris, or Frankfurt on Motor Road N-2 reach Zurich by way of its northern outskirts. Travelers arriving from Italy, Lugano, and the St. Gotthard Pass on Motor Road N-2 or from Chur in the Canton Grisons (Graubünden), western Austria, or the Principality of Liechtenstein on other highways enter the city from the south, along the left (west) bank of the lake. Directions to the city center from the exits of the motor roads and highways are well marked.

For assistance in a mechanical breakdown on the road, call 140 (Strassenhilfe). For other assistance, motorists turn to the Touring-Club Suisse (TCS), 38 Alfred-Escher-Strasse (2022122), on the west bank of the lake, or to Automobil-Club der Schweiz (ACS), 95 Forchstrasse (551500), on the east bank.

Motorists who have consumed more alcohol than is good for their own and other people's safety are advised to call 2724444 (Taxi-Zentrale), asking for Tandem Service; a second driver will be speedily dispatched to them.

For rental cars, look in the Zurich telephone directory under *Auto-Vermietungen*.

TRANSPORTATION

Mass transit throughout the city and its metropolitan region including the industrial city of Winterthur, 13 miles (nearly 21 kilometers) northeast of Zurich, is integrated into the Zurich Transit System (Zürcher Verkehrsverband, ZVV). (For information, call 3113939.) The network comprises the blue tramcars that crisscross the city center, trolley cars, buses, surface and underground lines of the new S-Bahn (Schnellbahn), private railways, a cableway, and lake boats. Tickets are issued for one or more of the forty-five tariff zones into which the system is divided, and entitle the holder to use all means of public transportation within the selected area with any number of transfers.

Buy tickets for trams and buses from vending machines at each stop, at Public Transport (ZVV) booths at various points in the city, or at railroad stations. No tickets are sold on trams or buses. Passengers found without a ticket during occasional checks are fined around $40 on the spot.

A short ride cost $1.25 in 1993, the ticket being valid for thirty minutes; the fare for a longer trip within city limits (up to two hours) was $2.15. Children between the ages of six and sixteen pay half price; those under six years of age travel free but must be accompanied by an adult.

The vending machines also dispense a wide array of tickets to the various tariff zones and give change. The machines are so elaborate that even some residents, especially senior citizens, are baffled and ask practiced bystanders for assistance. Newcomers may prefer to buy a twenty-four-hour ticket for the entire city network at $4.15, or for the whole region at $17, at the "ticketeria" in the rail terminal.

For objects left on trams or buses, apply to the city's Lost Property Office (Fundbüro), 10 Werdmühlestrasse (2165111), south of the main rail terminal (Hauptbahnhof).

Taxi ranks are outside the Hauptbahnhof and near major hotels. A cab ride from the main rail terminal to the Opera House, about a mile, costs around $9. For radio-dispatched cabs, call 2724444 or any other of the numbers listed under *Taxis* in the Zurich telephone directory. The numbers for wheelchair cabs are 2724242 and 2725040. For limousines, see the telephone directory under *Limousine Services*.

Sightseeing coaches with English-speaking guides leave for a two-hour city tour from the Tourist Information Office (2114000) on the south side of the main rail terminal (Hauptbahnhof) at 10 A.M. and 2 P.M. daily. The fare is $14. The Tourist Information Office also organizes walking tours through the Old Town on evenings during the warm months,

An antique tramcar of 1928 vintage rolls off for a nostalgic one-hour "Gold-timer" city tour on some afternoons between May and October. These tours depart from the Globus department store, Löwenplatz, southeast of the Hauptbahnhof. Fare, $9; information, 2114000.

Sightseeing boats seating forty passengers depart from a dock near the Swiss National Museum behind the Hauptbahnhof at thirty-minute intervals between 1 and 6 P.M. daily between the middle of April and the end of October; also every half hour from 10 A.M. to 1 P.M. Saturday and Sunday (daily in July and August). The boats sail up the Limmat under seven bridges to the Lake of Zurich, approach first the east shore and then the west shore, and return to the National Museum. Fare, $3.60; information, 4821033.

Tours of the Lake of Zurich are conducted in the large, white motorboats of the Lake Navigation Company (Zürichsee-Schiffahrtsgesellschaft); occasionally also in one of two restored historic paddle wheel steamers. Options range from a ninety-minute "short tour," taking place every day in the year, to a four-hour "grand tour" as far as the town of Rapperswil (p. 93) on the northeast shore, June to September. There is restaurant service on board, and on some evenings in the warm months "fondue tours" with music and dance are organized. The boats sail from the dock at Bürkliplatz at the southern end of Bahnhofstrasse, which can be reached by the No. 11 tram from Hauptbahnhof. For information, call 4821033.

ACCOMMODATIONS

More than one hundred hotels in Zurich and near its airport offer some thirteen thousand beds, most of them in rooms or suites with private bathrooms or showers. An additional eighteen hundred beds are available in smaller houses in the surroundings, 3.75 to 17.5 miles (6 to 28 kilometers) from the city center, several of them with a lake panorama.

An electronic signboard at the main rail terminal (Hauptbahnhof), at the head of the street-level platforms, indicates available space in a number of hotels belonging to different price categories. Push the appropriate button to place a free phone call to the reservation desk at the hotel of your choice.

Following is a list of outstanding hotels in each category (discussed on p. 15). Omissions do not imply any value judgment.

Five-star Houses ($225 to $385 for a double room, continental breakfast included)

Baur au Lac, 1 Talstrasse (2211650, fax 2118139), near the southern end of Bahnhofstrasse and the lakefront, overlooks the Schanzengraben, a canal that is a former moat and links the Sihl River with the lake.

An Austrian immigrant who rose from baker's apprentice to successful entrepreneur, Johannes Bauer, opened the establishment in 1844. The setting is an early nineteenth-century four-story townhouse in understated neoclassical style, with a portico and a small garden. The elegant establishment, renowned for its discreet, attentive service, is still owned by the founder's descendants. Royalty and other historic personages have been guests here, and Franz Liszt played the piano in its salon while Richard Wagner, who was later to become his son-in-law, sang from his own recent compositions.

The hotel's 210 beds are in rooms and suites with historic French or modern furniture. Grillwork balconies look out on the hotel garden and the lake. The Baur au Lac has three fine restaurants (p. 39) and a discotheque in a detached building across the canal. Its old wine shop, Weinhandlung Baur au Lac, 27 Börsenstrasse (2116380), at the back of the hotel, markets Swiss and imported vintages.

Dolder Grand Hotel, 65 Kurhausstrasse (2516231, fax 2518829), on a wooded slope, the Adlisberg, some 550 feet (183 meters) above the city and the lake, seems an exclusive Victorian country club, a holdover from the belle époque. The yellowish main structure, its ground plan suggesting a fan spread out in the direction of Zurich, is timber-framed with balconies, dormers, and three pagoda-shaped spiked towers.

The Dolder Grand opened in 1899; an annex in Riviera-

condo style with terraces and gaudy awnings was added to
the west wing in 1964. The extra-smooth service is in
keeping with the old-world aura. Churchill, Einstein, Tos-
canini, and other greats have been patrons. Suites and
rooms, all shielded by double doors, are spacious, with
sober neo-Empire furniture. There are 300 beds. Pine trees,
oaks, birches, and beeches can be seen from all windows,
and front rooms command a view of Zurich and the lake.
Guests enjoy free use of the nine-hole golf course, swimming pool, skating rink, and tennis court that are part of
the 50-acre (20-hectare) estate.

A cogwheel car departs from a terminal just above the
Dolder Grand every twenty minutes from early morning
to 11:30 P.M., delivering passengers at the Römerhof, a
square where tramlines converge (No. 3 to Hauptbahnhof,
No. 8 to the city center). Hotel guests travel free on the
cogwheel railway to and from Römerhof. The crescent-
shaped restaurant of the Dolder Grand, La Rotonde, with
picture windows looking out on the park, has French-
inspired cuisine and suave service.

Savoy Baur en Ville, am Paradeplatz (2115360, fax
2211467), off Bahnhofstrasse, is in the heart of the shopping and financial district. The first Zurich hotel of Johannes Bauer (p. 32), the building was erected in 1838,
renovated in art nouveau style in 1908, and rebuilt in 1978.
The Savoy Bauer en Ville offers elegant rooms and suites
with 150 beds, urbane service, and a bar that is popular
with business and banking types.

Eden au Lac, 45 Utoquai (2619404, fax 2619409), is a
relatively small house (seventy-five beds) in a domed neobaroque building on the lake's east shore that has been
designated a historic landmark. Opened in 1908, it has
retained the atmosphere of a leisurely era that a faithful

clientele appreciates. Since the Eden au Lac is close to the Opera House, artists and operagoers from out of town favor it. Sumptuous restaurant.

Zürich & La Résidence, 42 Neumühlequai (3636363, fax 3636015), on the east bank of the Limmat, not far from the rail terminal, is a big, modern establishment geared to the needs of business executives. There are 500 beds in the high-rise main building and in the annex. From the top floors the view embraces much of Zurich, the hills left and right, the Limmat River, and the lake. Service and restaurants are competent and somewhat impersonal.

Four-star Houses ($148 to $330 for a double room)

Bellerive au Lac, 47 Utoquai (2517010, fax 2514543), is next to the Eden au Lac (see p. 33) and has 80 beds. Quiet.

Central Plaza, 1 Central (2515555, fax 2518535), is across the Limmat from the Hauptbahnhof and has 135 beds. Family-run with personalized service.

Dolder Waldhaus, 20 Kurhausstrasse (2519360, fax 2510029), is close to the Dolder Grand (see p. 32) and has the same ownership. The 160-bed Waldhaus shares the country-club amenities of the larger establishment.

Schweizerhof, 7 Bahnhofplatz (2118640, fax 2113505), is opposite the main rail terminal. Opened in the late nineteenth century as the quintessential high-class railroad hotel, the 150-bed house has been thoroughly renovated. It is comfortable and has a business clientele.

Zum Storchen, 2 Weinplatz (2115510, fax 2116451), a rebuilt old inn in the heart of the Old Town, is near what in Roman times was a river pier. Some of the sixty rooms with 110 beds look out on the Limmat, others on the square, and still others on the narrow Storchengasse. The grill room is a much frequented meeting place.

Three-star Houses ($95 to $180 for a double room)

City, 34 Löwenstrasse (2112055, fax 2120036), near the main rail terminal and big department stores, is a modern no-nonsense establishment with small, functional rooms (100 beds) and an informal restaurant and bar. Quiet.

Sunnehus, 17 Sonneggstrasse (2516580, fax 2520268), is near the Federal Polytechnic College. Small (forty-six beds), plain, and friendly.

Zürcherhof, 21 Zähringerstrasse (2621040, fax 2620484), is in the Niederdorf section. Small (fifty beds) and comfortable.

Two-star Selection ($90 to $120 for a double room)

Limmathof, 142 Limmatquai (2614220, fax 2620217), on the east bank of the river, was recently renovated. It has 100 beds.

One-star Selection (around $80 for a double room)

Hirschen, 13 Niederdorfstrasse (2514252, fax 2514260), in the Niederdorf section, has sixty-two beds. Rooms without private bath and toilet are $57 for a double.

Apartment Hotels

Apartotel Hugenschmidt, 5 Karlstrasse (551175), is on

the eastern lakeshore. See also in the Zurich telephone directory under *Appartementhäuser.*

Hotels on Zurich's Outskirts

At **Küsnacht,** on the eastern lakeshore, 6.25 miles (10 kilometers) from the city center: **Ermitage,** 80 Seestrasse (9105222, fax 9105244), is a recently renovated four-star house with forty-three beds in double rooms, some with balconies, three singles, and cozy attic suites. Elegant restaurant, Le Pavillon, with garden and lake panorama. **Sonne,** 120 Seestrasse (9100201, fax 9100252), is a two-star hotel with thirty-six beds and a garden.

At **Obermeilen,** on the eastern lakeshore, 9.25 miles (15 kilometers) from the city center: **Hirschen,** 856 Seestrasse (9236551), three stars, is a 350-year-old inn with thirty-five beds, a good restaurant and tavern, and its own small harbor.

At **Thalwil,** on the western lakeshore, 6.25 miles (10 kilometers) from the city center: **Thalwilerhof,** 16 Bahnhofstrasse (7200603), two stars, is at the center of town. Good rail connections with Zurich.

See also **Rapperswil,** p. 93.

Rooms and Apartments

For short- and medium-term rentals, look for agents in the Zurich telephone directory under *Wohnungs- und Zimmeragenturen.* Also scan the real estate advertising sections of the local newspapers, especially *Tages-Anzeiger.*

Youth Hostel

Youth Hostel, 114 Mutschellenstrasse (4823544), in the Wollishofen section, is on the western lakeshore (No. 7 tram from Hauptbahnhof). It has 375 beds and is open all year for members of the International Youth Hostels Federation. Closed 9 A.M. to 2 P.M. daily.

Camping Sites

Seebucht, 557–559 Seestrasse (4821612), is in the Wollishofen section on the western lakeshore (No. 165 bus from Bürkliplatz at the south end of Bahnhofstrasse). On request, the management supplies addresses of other camping sites in the environs of Zurich.

EATING OUT

Zurich's cuisine is eclectic, while its basis is solidly Alemannic—sausages, pork, veal, potatoes, small dumplings, and sauerkraut. The nearby lakes and rivers still supply some freshwater fish, but most of those reaching Zurich tables come from hatcheries in various parts of Switzerland and in Germany. Culinary influences from the French-speaking western part of the country as well as from France, Italy, and Austria are strong. The city's thirteen hundred eating places include many French, Italian, Spanish, and Asian restaurants.

The few gastronomic specialties of Zurich are daily standbys in establishments from the *Beizen* (neighborhood taverns) to rathskeller-type guild houses. Foremost is *Geschnetzeltes*, minced and creamed veal. The tender meat

in its usually bland sauce comes ritually with *Rösti* (pronounced ROESH-tee), boiled and finely sliced potatoes
that were subsequently fried in pork fat (and perhaps a
little butter) and roasted. Golden Rösti, the all-purpose
Zurich side order, regularly also accompany St. Gall bratwurst, which is made of veal and customarily served also
with boiled onions.

Other popular meat dishes are *Kutteln*, the eatable parts
of a freshly slaughtered animal's intestines; *Metzgete*
(butchery platter), with blood sausage, liver sausage, and
the like; *Bernerplatte* (Bernese platter) with sausages, ham,
bacon, potatoes, and sauerkraut; and skewered calf's liver
with bacon and potatoes. Schnitzel and goulash, Austrian
and Hungarian style, are also familiar dishes. *Bündnerfleisch*
is raw, smoke-dried beef, finely sliced, in the style of Graubünden (Canton Grisons) southeast of Zurich. *Spätzle* (little sparrows), another frequent side order, are small
dumplings; *Leberknödel* (liver dumplings) are served in
bouillon, the Austrian way. Many eating places offer game
during the hunting season from autumn to spring. Plump
asparagus is a Zurich spring delicacy.

The freshwater fish, under such names as *Egli*, *Felche*,
Steinbutt, and *Zander*, belong to the pike-perch and turbot
families and are often served as fillets. Trout *(Forelle)* is
frequently on the menu, but the product probably comes
from fish farms rather than from a river fishery. Soles,
salmon, other sea fish, oysters, and crustaceans are flown
in daily from abroad and are available in the more sophisticated restaurants.

Cheeses are plentiful everywhere; at least a dozen different kinds, all of excellent quality, can be found on the
dairy counters of any supermarket. Fondue (compare p.
162) is available in many eating places in Zurich. The

substantial Italian presence in the city finds expression in the ubiquity of pasta dishes, risotto, and pizza. Favored desserts range from French-style chocolate mousse to rich Viennese and Hungarian tortes.

Many Zurichers are wine drinkers, even discriminating wine connoisseurs. Popular whites are Riesling Silvaner from the nearby Canton Schaffhausen or other wineries in eastern Switzerland, Dézaley and Aigle from the Canton Vaud, and Fendant from the Canton Valais. Red wines widely available in Zurich include Blauburgunder (the German term for Pinot Noir) from the eastern part of the country, Dôle from the Valais, and Merlot from the Italian-speaking Canton Ticino. Kirsch, the colorless brandy distilled from black cherries that is a specialty of the nearby Canton Zug, is a favorite liqueur.

Outstanding Restaurants in Hotels

The restaurants of some Zurich hotels through their cuisine, service, and decor also attract patrons who are not house guests. Outstanding are:

La Rotonde of the Dolder Grand Hotel (p. 32); the **Grill Room** of the Baur au Lac (p. 32); and the **Storchen-Rôtisserie** of the Hotel zum Storchen (p. 34). The cuisine in all three restaurants is French-inspired. Estimate around $50 a person for the fixed-price menus, up to $75 for à la carte dinners before wine. No carafe wines are served at La Rotonde, but half-bottles of some vintages are available.

On Zurich's outskirts: **Le Pavillon** at the Ermitage Hotel (p. 36) at Küsnacht, with French cuisine and a large wine list. Count on around $40 a person for lunch, with some open wine, $50 and up for dinner.

Top Restaurants

Such restaurants are closed on Sunday; some are also closed for lunch on Saturday or Monday.

Petermann's Kunststuben, 160 Seestrasse, Küsnacht (9100715), is a fifteen-minute trip on the S-7 Schnellbahn line from Hauptbahnhof to Küsnacht station and a short walk toward the lakeshore or a (rather expensive) cab ride from downtown. Horst and Iris Petermann from Hamburg were not yet forty years old when they arrived in Zurich in the 1980s and opened their own place on the posh "Gold Coast." Michelin's *Europe* guide quickly awarded Kunststuben (Art Rooms) a star, and in 1986 a second one, thus making it the first Zurich restaurant found worthy of such a French accolade.

Adjoining a small, private art gallery, the L-shaped restaurant has a low ceiling, a majolica-tile stove, and round tables with immaculate linen and a profusion of fresh flowers. Guests for lunch and, especially, dinner reserve weeks ahead. Most patrons follow the suggestions of the handwritten fixed-price menu, which is in French. Petermann's cooking is modified nouvelle cuisine, creative and perfectionist. He uses coriander, fennel, and ginger to spice his fish dishes; his roast saddle of lamb is a triumph; his mille-feuilles cake with chocolate and pears is only one of several superlative desserts. Complete menus are around $125 a person; the three-course menu is $100; the menu surprise, consisting of six to eight courses, is $140.

Closer to the city center: **Chez Max,** 53 Seestrasse (3918877), is in the Zollikon section on the eastern lakeshore. Max A. Kehl introduced nouvelle cuisine to Zurich in the late 1970s and later experimented with Japanese-style cooking. His elegant restaurant and bar, closed for lunch except on Saturday, serves imaginative French-oriented dishes such as lobster salad in vodka sauce or slice of turbot with saffron seeds; refined desserts and sherbets; the wines are mostly French. Dinner costs about $150 per person including wine.

Agnes Amberg, 5 Hottingerstrasse (2512626), near the Kunsthaus, was opened in the 1970s by a female chef, food writer, and teacher of cookery classes. Mrs. Amberg died in 1991, but her heirs are attempting to maintain her high standards. Opulent decor and excellent service. Four-course luncheon menus start at $40 a person before wines. An $80 gourmet meal for weight watchers (two persons at least) is composed of five courses totaling a guaranteed "997 calories or 4,173 joules," as the menu scientifically states.

Kronenhalle, 4 Rämistrasse (2510256), near the Quay Bridge and the Opera House, is a 130-year-old Zurich institution. The writer and poet Gottfried Keller, a Swiss icon, was a regular, and James Joyce drank his beloved Fendant wine there. Today artists, intellectuals, and industrialists as well as media and fashion people crowd the restaurant's dark-paneled rooms and its bar. Original pictures by Braque, Chagall, Miró, and Picasso hang on the walls. The cuisine is a blend of Alemannic and French— *Geschnetzeltes* and St. Gall bratwurst are always on the menu, as are fresh fish and seafood. For dessert, many habitués ask for the house specialty, chocolate mousse, spooned out of chilled containers in front of the patrons. Good open wines. Count on at least $45 a person for lunch, with two deciliters of Swiss or French wine. The service is brisk.

Baron de la Mouette, 18 Dreikönigstrasse (2020910), near the southern end of Bahnhofstrasse, is the flagship of the Mövenpick restaurant and hotel chain (*mouette* is French for the German word *Möve*, which means *gull*). In showy decor, Baron de la Mouette may resemble the other Mövenpick units around town (some twenty of them) and in other parts of Switzerland, but the cuisine is more inventive, the service more cordial. French seafood daily; the impressive wine list includes Californian vintages. About $35 a person for lunch or dinner.

Kaiser's Reblaube und Goethe-Stübli, 7 Glockengasse (2212120), is in the Old Town between Bahnhofstrasse and the Limmat. The much-photographed frescoed facade shows the portraits of Goethe and his princely employer, Duke Karl August of Weimar, who together in 1779 visited Johann Kaspar Lavater, the Zurich preacher and physiognomist, in this building. A rhymed inscription in Goethe's German urges visitors not to linger outside but to step in to a friendly welcome. Service is indeed pleasant, and the cuisine is in the traditional Zurich way. Good wine list. Lunch or dinner with some open wine is approximately $50 a person.

Guild Houses

Zurich's medieval craftsmen's and merchants' guilds live on in folklore parades (p. 82) and through their former headquarters, several of which have been restored or rebuilt. Comfortable and perhaps a little staid taverns and restaurants, with vaulted ceilings and plenty of wainscoting, have long taken over the old buildings. The food is usually Alemannic-substantial, and beer flows; open wines are also served. A filling, unsophisticated lunch or dinner needn't cost more than $50 a person; plat du jour alone or snacks up to $25. All guild houses listed below are open also Sunday.

Zunfthaus zum Rüden, 42 Limmatquai (2619566), near City Hall, is in a seven-hundred-year-old arcaded edifice that through the centuries has been repeatedly altered; the city's merchant nobility once used to meet here. A historic landmark. The restaurant stresses "market cuisine," meaning it uses fresh, seasonal supplies.

Zunfthaus zur Saffran, 54 Limmatquai (2616565), near City Hall, is in a frowning structure from the fourteenth century with an arcade and stuccoed rooms. The building has been designated a historic landmark. Traditional Zurich fare is served in the main restaurant on the second floor, while the "Risotteria" on the ground floor, open until midnight, specializes in Italian rice dishes.

Zunfthaus zur Schmieden, 20 Marktgasse (2515287), near City Hall, is in a medieval building with an impressive third-floor hall (only for banquets). The attractive second-floor restaurant serves French and Zurich dishes, fish, and game.

Zunfthaus zur Waag, 8 Münsterhof (2110730), is in an attractive square between Paradeplatz and the Limmat. The old headquarters of weavers and hatters was rebuilt in 1936 with a smiling baroque facade; flowers and blue-yellow ribbons are in all the windows. Zurich specialties and, in season, game.

Accent on Beer

Zeughauskeller, 28A Bahnhofstrasse (2112690), is in a former civic arsenal and has a central location. As a result, it is somewhat touristy, with menus in several languages.

Sausages, potato salad, roast pig, and other Alemannic treats are served. Lunch or dinner with beer, around $40 a person; open wines are also available.

Bierhalle Kropf, 16 In Gassen (2211805), off Paradeplatz, has Bavarian Jugendstil (art nouveau) decor and beer garden food. A house specialty is the selection from the steam table. Lunch and dinner menu, $15 and up.

Brasserie Lipp, 2 Uraniastrasse (2111155), off Bahnhofstrasse, was opened in 1991 on the ground floor and on the top of the 150-foot (45-meter) astronomical observatory of the cantonal adult-education institute Urania. It features *choucroûte garnie*, cassoulet, and other brasserie food as at Lipp's on Boulevard St. Germain in Paris. The panoramic Jules Verne Bar on top of the tower serves snacks and is often reserved for private parties. Count on $25 to $30 a person for lunch with beer; wines are served as well.

James Joyce Pub, 6 Pelikanstrasse (2211828), in the financial district west of Bahnhofstrasse, is a piece of old Dublin transplanted to Zurich. The Victorian decor of the place is that of the bar in Dublin's defunct Jury's Hotel on Dane Street. Jury's Antique Bar is mentioned in *Ulysses*, and Joyce is believed to have drunk in it once in a while as a young man. When the old Jury's Hotel was razed in the early 1970s, the Union Bank of Switzerland bought the bar furnishings in an auction and shipped them to Zurich. The 35-foot (11-meter) dark wood counter of the old Jury's, its bar stools, wine-red settees, octagonal tables topped with black-and-white marble, mosaic floor, stained-glass windows, and allegorical wall tiles have become a Zurich curiosity. The short menu offers "Mr. Bloom's Breakfast," the veal kidneys on toast with tea (or Guinness stout) on which the hero of *Ulysses* doted. Also fish and chips, hamburgers, and other snacks. Swiss and imported beers, whiskeys, and open wines. Pleasant service. Light lunch with beer, $15 to $20 a person. Open 10:30 A.M. to 11 P.M. Monday to Friday, 7 to 11 P.M. Saturday.

French-Swiss Cuisine

Dézaley Cave Vaudoise, 7 Römergasse (2516129), near the Grossmünster Cathedral, is named after a renowned vintage from the Lausanne region and serves fondues, freshwater fish fillets, and other specialties of the French-speaking part of Switzerland. Attractive garden.

Fish Restaurants

La Bouillabaisse, 87 Bahnhofstrasse (2118317), near the main rail terminal (Hauptbahnhof), is one of the restaurants of the four-star St. Gotthard Hotel. Catches from the Atlantic and the Mediterranean arrive by air daily. The specialty is Marseille-style bouillabaisse with lobster, up to $55; other fish dishes cost around $30. Under the same roof: **Hummer- und Austernbar,** with entrance at 14 Linthescherjasse (2118315), is an intimate, expensive place for lobster, oysters, and other seafood.

Fisherman's Lodge Seerestaurant, 61 Mythenquai (2020280), on the western lakeshore, has a terrace overlooking the water. Exotic maritime decor, sea- and freshwater fish. Lunch or dinner with some wine, from $35 a person.

Italian Restaurants

Piccoli-Accademia, 48 Rotwandstrasse (2416243), in a lower-middle-class neighborhood west of the Sihl River, is not far from Hauptbahnhof. On the large menu are many pasta and risotto varieties; also excellent steaks. Several northern Italian vintages are on the wine list. Lunch or dinner about $40 a person.

Casa Ferlin Chiantiquelle, 38 Stampfenbachstrasse (3623509), is on the east bank of the Limmat near Central Square. One of the oldest of Zurich's many Italian eating places, this is also among the more expensive. Its ravioli are famous; its house wine is satisfactory Chianti. Pleasant decor and service. Count on $50 a person for dinner.

Spanish Cooking

Ribó, 43 Luisenstrasse (2724864), is near the west bank of the Limmat and Hauptbahnhof. Catalan cuisine in a small, friendly place with moderate prices. A perennial hit is roast chicken, grandmother style *(pollo abuelita)* with potatoes, small onions, and garlic. Also paella. The house wine is Rioja. Lunch or dinner, $35 to $40.

Asian Food

China Town, 65 Hotzestrasse (3611655), east of the Limmat, is near Schaffhauserplatz. Cantonese cuisine with excellent wonton; also Peking duck, scampi. Chinese beer, green tea, and wines. The large second-floor restaurant is open on Sunday, closed Monday. Lunch menu starts at $17.

Fujiya of Japan, 5 Tessinerplatz (2011155), near the western lakeshore, is not far from the southern end of Bahnhofstrasse. Europeanized Japanese cuisine: sashimi, diced steak, fried rice. Menu, from $40 a person, before sake or wine.

Sala of Tokyo, 29 Limmatstrasse (2715290), is off the
west bank of the Limmat near Hauptbahnhof. The small
menu lists sashimi, sukiyaki, tempura, and a few other
traditional Japanese dishes. Elegantly sober Japanese ambiance. Count on $50 a person for lunch or dinner.

Kosher Restaurant

Café Shalom, 33 Lavaterstrasse (2011476), is off the western lakeshore in the Enge section, in the building of the
Zurich Rabbinate and Jewish Community. This restaurant
features typical kosher cuisine, which will cost approximately $30 per person.

Moderately Priced and Informal

Mère Catherine, 3 Nägelihof, Rüdenplatz (2622250), is
near the Grossmünster Cathedral. This bistro on two levels
attracts young people and is often crowded. The cuisine is
unsophisticated: lamb and fish fillets, curried "Mère Catherine" salad, minced veal, and liver. Open French wines
and good espresso. Lunch and dinner menus from $20,
also snacks. Open 11:30 A.M. to 11:45 P.M. daily. Night-
caps and onion soup in the adjoining small **Bar Le Philo-
sophe.**

Vorderer Sternen, 22 Theaterstrasse (2514949), near
Bellevue-Platz and the Opera House, is a popular restaurant in the one-star hotel of the same name. Vast selection
of grilled sausages, boiled meat, chicken, and vegetarian
dishes. Terrace and covered garden. Snacks and full meals,
$10 to $30. Open 11:30 A.M. to 11:30 P.M. daily.

Bier-Falken, 16 Löwenstrasse (2116823), on a shopping
street near Hauptbahnhof, offers typical Zurich treats and

beer. Warm dishes are served from 11 A.M. to 11 P.M. Monday to Friday, 11 A.M. to 6 P.M. Saturday. Often crowded. Lunch menu from $12.

MIGROS Restaurants, operated by the cooperative chain, are inexpensive eating places in various parts of the city. One of them is in MIGROS's City MMM branch, 31-35 Löwenstrasse (2115978), near Hauptbahnhof, and is open during business hours. For other locations, look up *Migros-Genossenschaft Zürich* in the telephone directory.

Railroad Station Food

Hauptbahnhof Restaurants, at the main rail terminal (2111510), is a cluster of eateries that includes an economical **Rösti Bar** (compare p. 38) on the ground floor off the old concourse; a brasserie; a café; and the French-inspired **Au Premier** on the second floor, one of Europe's better railroad-station restaurants. If you spurn the Rösti Bar, the best deal will be found in the ground-floor brasserie, open 11 A.M. to 11 P.M. daily.

Fast Food

McDonald's has branches at 79 Bahnhofstrasse (2210919), and at 30 Niederdorfstrasse (2529930) in the Niederdorf section.

Burger King, 12 Schützengasse (2117100), is near Hauptbahnhof.

Many snack bars and pizzerias are located around the main rail terminal and in the Niederdorf section. Sausage and sandwich stands are to be found outside the department stores and at various points in the city center during shopping hours as well as at the main rail terminal from early morning to late at night.

Wine Bar

Caveau Mövenpick Wine Pub, 1 Nüschelerstrasse (2119139), is in the financial district between Bahnhofstrasse and the Sihl River. This wainscoted place is for wine lovers and connoisseurs, who may select from a large number of Swiss, French, Italian, Spanish, and Californian vintages. Soups, salads, salmon sandwiches, roast beef, and spaghetti go with the wine. Count on $30 for a couple of glasses of a medium-price vintage and a snack. Open 11:30 A.M. to 11:30 P.M. Monday to Saturday.

Coffee and Chocolate

Sprüngli, 21 Bahnhofstrasse (2211722), off Paradeplatz, has been a famous chocolate and pastry shop since the middle of the nineteenth century. Excellent espresso and cappuccino are served in its corner bar on the ground floor next to the store with tempting pralines, chocolate truffles, cakes, and tortes. The refreshment rooms upstairs serve ravioli, salads, sandwiches, and other snacks. Closed on Sundays. Sprüngli has branches at the main rail terminal, at Kloten Airport, and at a few other locations around the city.

Café Schober, 4 Napfgasse (2518060), with a terrace on a lane near Grossmünster Cathedral, has been in business since 1842 and is now owned by the Teuscher chocolate firm. Famous hot chocolate, good coffee, and fine pastry. The historic place is often crowded with aficionados and is a favorite haunt for Sunday brunch.

Café Odeon, 2 Limmatquai (2511650), near Bellevue-
Platz, was once popular with artists and writers. Lenin,
James Joyce, Somerset Maugham, Stefan Zweig, Richard
Strauss, and Thomas Mann were often seen here. Upstairs,
at the "Little Odeon," the Dutch-Indonesian spy Marga-
retha Geertruida Zelle, better remembered as Mata Hari,
used to dance. Open until 2 A.M., weeknights, 4 A.M.
Friday and Saturday.

Picnic Food

In addition to the food sections of Globus, Jelmoli, and
other department stores, and the many branches of the
COOP and MIGROS chains (p. 48 and Zurich telephone
directory), a good place to buy cold cuts, sausages, cheeses,
and other snacks is **Picnic,** 52 Bahnhofstrasse (2119283).

WHAT TO SEE

The center of Zurich is so compact and relatively small
that its principal sights—except the museums—can be visited on foot or by streetcar in a few hours. The Bahnhofstrasse, more or less parallel to the Limmat River, bisects
the city from north to south. To the east, between the
glamorous boulevard and the river, is the oldest section of
Zurich, which goes back to antiquity. The medieval Old
Town clusters on either side of the Limmat close to the
lake.

West of Bahnhofstrasse are modern districts, which
house the headquarters of large banks. Farther west, across
the Sihl River and northwest of the main rail terminal
(Hauptbahnhof), are industrial and lower-middle-class
sections of little interest to sightseers. Zurich skirts the

northern end of its lake with stately buildings, well-tended promenades, and chic suburbs. Residential neighborhoods have since the end of the nineteenth century crept up the hills east of the lake and the Limmat; they can easily be reached by public transport, but a visitor with limited time needn't bother.

Zurich's Modern Core

To many visitors, including some who arrive in the city periodically to do business or just look after their bank portfolios and rented safes, Zurich is essentially the **Bahnhofstrasse.** The broad avenue, lined with linden trees, runs from the main rail terminal in a slight arc to the lakeshore at Bürkliplatz. The Bahnhofstrasse is not quite a mile (1.5 kilometers) long, but a stroller may spend a couple of hours getting from one end to the other, perhaps doing window-shopping and stopping to rest at one of several café terraces. The Bahnhofstrasse is closed to private motor traffic for long stretches; pedestrians walk freely in the middle of this street—but watch out for the blue streetcars.

Several of Zurich's large department stores are on or off the Bahnhofstrasse. They and a great number of other retail businesses and boutiques make the boulevard the city's principal shopping street (p. 90).

The heart of Bahnhofstrasse and of modern Zurich is the **Paradeplatz,** so named because it once served for exercises of the citizens' militia. Six tramlines converge in this irregularly shaped square. The country's three biggest banks—Union Bank of Switzerland, Swiss Bank Corporation, and Crédit Suisse—have their central offices on, or close to, Paradeplatz. Other bank buildings are nearby. Electronic signboards in the show windows of the financial institutions flash the latest quotations of the Zurich Stock

Exchange and from Wall Street as well as the day's exchange rates of the U.S. dollar and other foreign curren-
cies. The Zurich Stock Exchange (Effektenbörse) is west
of the Paradeplatz, at 32 Selnauer Strasse (2292233). The
Zurich branch of the Swiss National Bank, which has its
headquarters in Bern, is a soberly dignified building at the
southern end of Bahnhofstrasse, with its entrance at 15
Börsenstrasse (2213750).

Bahnhofstrasse and Paradeplatz are the realm of what
Lord George-Brown, Britain's foreign secretary before he
became a peer, called "the gnomes of Zurich"—the bankers and financiers of the Swiss metropolis. The character-
ization, resented as invidious by its targets, may have been
based on the fact that some of the bank safes are underground. It is, however, just a myth that a treasure of gold
ingots is stashed deep below Bahnhofstrasse. Some of Zurich's bank safes above and below ground level are so large
that depositors can enter them when the steel doors are
opened. Works of art and other bulky valuables are kept
in such walk-in caches. The tribe of the Zurich "gnomes"
is not exclusively Swiss: business signs of American, Japanese, Arabic, and other foreign financial institutions may
be spotted along Bahnhofstrasse and in its surroundings.

Few people live on Bahnhofstrasse and in the business
district between it and the Sihl River. After office and
shopping hours and on weekends, the entire neighborhood, which Zurichers call the "City" (using the English
term), looks deserted.

The Old Town

Walking down Bahnhofstrasse from the main rail terminal,
turn left into the broad Rennweg, a shopping street, and

again left into the curving Fortunagasse. It skirts a hill,
some 60 feet (20 meters) above the Limmat. Known as the
Lindenhof, the hill is a moraine, a heap of stones and earth
pushed up by an Ice Age glacier. The ancient Romans
installed on it a customs station under Emperor Augustus
(about 15 B.C.) and in the fourth century A.D. built a forti-
fied military camp with a tower. The Roman name of the
spot, Turicum (stress the middle syllable, pronouncing it
REE), was probably derived from a Celtic word or proper
name, and over the centuries it became Zurich. In the early
Middle Ages the area's Carolingian overlords had a castle
(*Pfalz*, or palace) built on the hill. Ruins of the Roman and
medieval structures have been dug up.

Today the Lindenhof is a park with plane trees and a
terrace looking out on the opposite bank of the Limmat
with the cathedral (Grossmünster, p. 56), the academic
buildings (p. 59), and the eastern hills. In the park there is
a children's playground and a seventy-year-old fountain
with a female figure commemorating the legendary cour-
age of Zurich's womenfolk during a siege of the city in
A.D. 1292.

On the southern edge of the square, at 4 Lindenhof-
strasse, is the headquarters of a masonic organization, the
Grand Lodge Alpina (2111349; no information by telephone). The nineteenth-century building looks Gothic and
indeed incorporates tracery salvaged from medieval structures. Walking south along narrow, ancient lanes—Pfalzgasse and Schlüsselgasse—you reach a quiet square, **St.
Peterhofstatt,** bordered by narrow houses. On its south
side rises the oldest surviving parish church of Zurich, **St.
Peter's.** It goes back to the eighth century and was rebuilt
several times; the Romanesque square tower is from the
thirteenth century. Zurichers will tell you that the four

clock faces of the steeple are the largest in Europe, which
they well may be—the minute hands are 12 feet (4 meters)
long.

Proceed farther south, past restored old buildings, to a
large square of irregular shape, **Münsterhof.** It is surrounded by old burgher and guild houses. Among the
latter is the **Zunfthaus zur Waag** (Guild House at the Sign
of the Balance, the symbol of the pharmacists who at one
time used to meet there); it stands out by its colorful facade
(compare p. 43). At the east side of the square is the **Zunfthaus zur Meisen** (Guild House at the Sign of the Tit-
mouse), the most sumptuous of the old city's corporation
buildings. It was erected in the French-baroque style in the
eighteenth century for the rich guild of the wine merchants,
with its main front facing the Limmat. The Zunfthaus zur
Meisen is at present the seat of the ceramics collection of
the Swiss National Museum (p. 62).

The south side of the square is taken up by the **Fraumünster,** a church that had its origin in an aristocratic
women's convent founded in A.D. 853 by a grandson of
Charlemagne (*Fraumünster* means *ladies' minster*). What is
seen today is an often-rebuilt Romanesque-Gothic edifice
from the thirteenth century and a tall steeple with large
clock faces and a needle roof. The old church was completely restored at the beginning of the twentieth century.

In 1968 the Reformed congregation of the Fraumünster, financially backed by anonymous sponsors, commissioned Marc Chagall, who was then eighty years old, to
design stained-glass windows for the renovated choir of
the church. The five windows, executed after Chagall's
designs by a workshop in Reims, France, are today a major
sightseeing attraction.

Four of the tall windows are devoted to the themes of

the Jewish tradition: the Prophets of Israel (dominant color, red); Jacob's Dream (blue); David, King of Zion (yellow); and Moses and the Law (blue). The central window, taller and somewhat broader than the other four, represents Mary, Joseph, and the Crucified and Resurrected Jesus (green). Stained-glass windows in the transept are by Augusto Giacometti (1945).

The Fraumünster is open 9 A.M. to noon and 2 to 6 P.M. Monday through Saturday, and 2 to 6 P.M. Sunday. Admission is free. On some evenings concerts take place in the church (watch for notices at the entrance).

The remains of a Romanesque cloister adjacent to the south side of the Fraumünster are now a public passageway with frescoes by the Swiss artist Paul Bodmer (1938), leading to the **Stadthaus** (City House). Facing the Limmat, the Stadthaus is a neo-Gothic edifice built in 1898–1900 on the site of the early-medieval women's convent. It is the seat of municipal offices and is also used for temporary exhibitions (p. 72).

Turn around and walk downstream along the Limmat, past the main facade of the Zunfthaus zur Meisen. The picturesque **Wühre** is a narrow embankment with a few cafés and fine views of the old city. It will take you to **Weinplatz** (Wine Square), which two thousand years ago was a dock for lake- and riverboats.

In more recent times wine used to be traded in the square, hence its name. The cast-iron, neobaroque **Vintner's Fountain** at the center was unveiled in 1908. The renowned **Inn at the Sign of the Sword** (Gasthaus zum Schwert) at No. 10 used to put up many prominent guests over the centuries, including Czar Alexander I of Russia and other royalty; Leopold Mozart with his children, Wolfgang Amadeus and Nannerl; Goethe; Victor Hugo; Liszt;

and Brahms. The broad **City Hall Bridge** (Rathaus-brücke) connecting Weinplatz with the opposite bank was opened in 1972, replacing an older structure.

Proceed northward from Weinplatz along the ancient river wharf known as **Schipfe.** The narrow houses, five and six stories high, between the Limmat and the Lindenhof hill are from the sixteenth to the eighteenth centuries. The flavor of a nordic little Venice lingers in the neighborhood with its arcades and narrow passageways. The Schipfe ends at the busy, broad **Uraniastrasse,** an important east-west artery named after a towered adult-education building.

The Major Town

From the eleventh century onward, the city of Zurich reached across the Limmat, and new neighborhoods developed on the river's right (east) bank that were eventually to be known as the Major Town, whereas the oldest districts on the west bank were called Lesser Zurich.

The **Grossmünster,** the cathedral of Zurich and its principal landmark, is the nucleus of the old district on the east bank. It is about 600 feet (200 meters) from the Fraumünster (p. 54) across the Münster Bridge. The two churches on either bank of the river with their steeples and spires seem to be carrying on an unending architectural dialogue.

The Grossmünster was built between the eleventh and thirteenth centuries; the two square Romanesque-Gothic towers were crowned in the late eighteenth century with octagonal metal-plated domes. The side of the south tower facing outward carries a sculpture of Charlemagne seated, a sword on his knee. According to tradition, Charlemagne had founded a collegiate church—one ruled by a chapter of canons—at the site where the cathedral was later to rise. The statue on the tower is a copy of the fifteenth-century sculpture in the church's crypt.

The interior of the Grossmünster is severe, with three naves. The large crypt is believed to mark the spot where the three early-Christian martyrs Saint Felix, Saint Regula (brother and sister), and their servant Saint Exuperantius were buried in the third century. The three legendary Romans are revered as Zurich's patron saints.

The Protestant Reformer Huldrych (Ulrich) Zwingli preached in the cathedral from 1518 to shortly before his death. He died in 1531 in a battle at Kappel near the city of Zug, south of Zurich, during a civil war with the Roman Catholic cantons. Zurich remained Protestant, and the Grossmünster is to this day the city's principal Reformed church.

Modern, narrow stained-glass windows are by Augusto Giacometti (1932–33). The Grossmünster can be visited from 10 A.M. to 4 P.M. Monday to Saturday, and on Sunday after services until 4 P.M. Admission is free.

The steep **Kirchgasse** (Church Lane) rises from the cathedral to what was once a moat (Hirschengraben). Note the old houses with bay windows on Kirchgasse; Zwingli lived at No. 13. The section south of Kirchgasse as far as the much-traveled Rämistrasse (p. 60) is known as **Oberdorf** (Upper Village). It is a neighborhood of modernized old houses, some with oriels and a few with little gardens, a quaint enclave.

Walk back to the cathedral and the Münster Bridge. Adjoining the bridge, close by the river, is a late-Gothic edifice, the **Wasserkirche** (Water Church). It was built in 1479–84 on what was then a small island in the river, the spot where, according to tradition, the city's patron saints were beheaded on orders from an official of the Roman

Emperor Decius. The old island has long been connected
with the right (east) riverbank. Adjacent to the Wasserkirche is the **Helmhaus,** now an exhibition hall (p. 73).

Strolling downstream, the visitor sees on the river-
front, close to the next bridge (Rathausbrücke), Zurich's
dignified **City Hall.** The baroque building from the end
of the seventeenth century, with dormer windows on its
curved roof, is the sumptuous seat of the city and cantonal
parliaments. A low building, pillared like a Greek temple,
facing City Hall from the other side of the bridgehead is
the **Hauptwache** (Main Guard), a police station. It was
built in 1824 when classical-revival architecture was the
fashion all over Europe.

The sloping **Spiegelgasse,** starting near (east of) City
Hall, doesn't look as if it played a part in European political
and intellectual history in the early twentieth century. But
it most certainly did. At No. 14 Lenin and his wife,
Nadezhda Krupskaya, roomed for fourteen months in the
grungy apartment of a shoemaker until the German government allowed them to travel to St. Petersburg in a sealed
railroad coach in April 1917. The building in which Lenin
lived has since been replaced by a new construction.

At a café at 1 Spiegelgasse that no longer exists, a group
of pacifist artists and writers at the height of World War I
in 1916 started the dadaist movement, a nihilistic revolt
against traditional values that was eventually to beget sur-
realism and other currents in modern art. An important
dadaist collection is at the Kunsthaus (Art House) (p. 64).

Near City Hall is a cluster of old **guild houses** (compare p. 42): Zunfthaus zur Zimmerleuten, 40 Limmatquai;
Zum Rüden, 42 Limmatquai; and Zur Saffran, 54 Limmatquai. From the High Middle Ages onward, the massive,
arcaded meeting places of craftsmen and merchants were
again and again rebuilt, restored, connected with nearby

structures, and embellished with stucco work, reliefs, and other ornaments. Eventually quite a few of them became restaurants.

From the guild houses and City Hall proceed north-ward past more than a dozen short alleys that connect the embankment (Limmatquai) with **Niederdorfstrasse,** the main drag of a bohemian district. The **Niederdorf** (Lower Village) is a center of Zurich late-night activities, with scores of cafés, restaurants, cabarets, and night spots (p. 81). When the elegant Bahnhofstrasse across the river gets quiet around 7 P.M., the Niederdorf comes to life.

The long Niederdorfstrasse, from which motor traffic is banned, leads to **Central,** a busy square where eight tram- and bus lines meet. Across the river, connected with Central by the Bahnhofbrücke (Station Bridge), is the main rail terminal (Hauptbahnhof).

The Zurich of Arts and Sciences

A chain of prestigious institutions in a wide arc from the academic district to the western lakeshore serves culture and learning. Their impressive buildings are emblems of the city's importance as an intellectual center.

The lake end of Bahnhofstrasse at Bürkliplatz is a con-venient starting point for exploring the Zurich of the arts and sciences. Only 600 feet (200 meters) to the right, on the lakeshore, is the **Kongresshaus,** a convention and con-ference complex that incorporates what has remained of the old **Tonhalle,** the city's principal concert hall.

The original Tonhalle was built in the last decade of the nineteenth century in a florid Moorish-baroque style inspired by the then new Trocadéro in Paris (which also was later reconstructed). At the inauguration of the ornate Zurich concert hall in 1895, Brahms conducted his *Trium-*

phant Song for choir, baritone, and orchestra, opus 55. In 1939 the lakefront part of the building was razed and replaced by the present Kongresshaus (entrances from General-Guisan-Quai and 5 Gotthardstrasse; 2016688). The two halls of the old Tonhalle, seating respectively 1,546 and 636 persons, were saved. The opulent Large Hall, with glittering chandeliers hanging from the frescoed ceiling, is renowned for its good acoustics. Some concert or recital takes place at the Tonhalle almost daily from October to the end of June (p. 79). The main entrance to the concert wing is at 7 Claridenstrasse.

Turn around and walk to the eastern lakeshore over the iron Quaibrücke (Quay Bridge). It commands a splendid view of the lake, of the hillside suburbs left and right, and, in clear weather, of the Glarus Alps some 30 miles (50 kilometers) to the southeast. Looking northward, one sees the Limmat flowing out of the lake, tribes of swans, ducks, and gulls that gather in the initial reach of the river, the twin towers of the Grossmünster, and the steeples and roofscape of the Old Town on the left bank.

The Quaibrücke takes the stroller to **Bellevue-Platz,** a traffic hub and one of Zurich's liveliest spots.

A little to the south is the **Opernhaus** (Opera House), facing the Kongresshaus and Tonhalle across the lake. The neobaroque Opera House was inaugurated in 1891 at the site of a theater that had burned down. More than ninety years later, in 1982–84, Zurich restored, modernized, and expanded its Opera House, joining to it a low-slung annex containing dressing and rehearsal rooms, workshops, a 450-seat theater (Bernhard Theater), and a restaurant (Belcanto, 2516951). The Opera House has 1,230 seats.

Returning to Bellevue-Platz, walk up the broad **Rämi-strasse** or take the No. 5, No. 8, or No. 9 tram to Heimplatz. At the beginning of Rämistrasse are two historic

hangouts of Swiss and international artists and intellectuals:
on the left, at 2 Limmatquai, is the **Café Odeon** (p. 50),
and on the right, 4 Rämistrasse, the **Kronenhalle** (p. 41).

Heimplatz is a large, triangular square. At its right is
the **Schauspielhaus** (Drama House). The 995-seat theater
at 34 Rämistrasse, which opened in 1884, won international fame during World War II. It was then the sole
German-language stage where works by Jewish and other
refugees from Nazi Germany could be performed. The
south side of Heimplatz and a stretch of Rämistrasse are
taken up by the large complex of the **Kunsthaus,** which
contains one of Europe's major art collections (p. 64).

Proceeding along the curving Rämistrasse (No. 5 and
No. 8 trams), the visitor passes various schools. Nearby,
at 6 Florhofgasse, is the **Zurich Conservatory and Music
College** (p. 79).

The Rämistrasse ends at the imposing academic district.
Here, on a ledge of the Zürichberg, some 120 feet (40
meters) above the Limmat, the domed buildings of Zurich
University and the Federal Polytechnic College rise side by
side. A terrace in front of the academic edifices commands a
sweeping panorama of Zurich, the lake, and the hills to the
west.

Zurich University (officially, Zurich University Center; "Uni" to its students) was built in 1914 by the architect
Karl Moser of Baden (near Zurich). Its terraced, square
tower with its metal cupola is 213 feet (68 meters) high.

North of the university, across the Künstlergasse (Artists' Lane), is the **Federal Polytechnic College,** often
referred to by the letters *ETH*, the initials of its official
German name, Eidgenössische Technische Hochschule
(Zurichers also call it the "Poly"). Among its many outstanding professors was Albert Einstein, who taught theo-
retical physics from 1909 to 1913. Gottfried Semper, who

was the institution's first professor of architecture, designed the original neo-Renaissance building in 1864. The structure was enlarged, and its center was crowned with a circular dome, in 1914–25.

Both the university and the polytechnic have branches and institutes in other parts of the city.

The academic district is linked with the lower city by stairways, sloping streets, and a **cable railway** between Central square and the northwest corner of the polytechnic at Leonhardstrasse. Affectionately known as the "Polybahn," the more than one-hundred-year-old conveyance is used not only by students but also by many people who live in the upper neighborhoods. Departures are every five or ten minutes from early morning to late at night. The ride costs about 60¢, but regulars use season tickets. The cable railway does not belong to the municipal transit system.

East of the university and the polytechnic is the large complex of the **University Hospital** (also known as the Cantonal Hospital), main entrance at 100 Rämistrasse, with specialized departments and clinics (p. 87).

Museums and Collections

Most of the institutions listed here are closed on Monday. If not otherwise stated, they are accessible to wheelchair users.

Swiss National Museum (Schweizerisches Landesmuseum), 2 Museumstrasse (2211010), is at the northeast side of the main rail terminal (Hauptbahnhof) and can be reached from it by an underpass. Open 10 A.M. to 5 P.M. Tuesday to Sunday. Free admission. Snacks and drinks are available at a refreshment tent in the museum courtyard.

The building, with its Gothic towers, dormers, and large showroom windows, looks like a cross between a medieval castle and a baroque palace, reflecting the Victorian predilection for mixing architectural elements from various epochs. It was opened in 1898. The vast collections of the museum are a visual encyclopedia of Swiss culture and history from the Stone Age to about the nineteenth century.

There are prehistoric and pre-Roman artifacts; plenty of ancient Roman pottery and other objects; Romanesque and Gothic art; works by medieval and Renaissance craftsmen; furniture from the fifteenth to the eighteenth centuries (including completely equipped rooms); tile stoves; textiles and costumes from various eras; silverware; clocks; and coins.

A Hall of Weapons with armor, crossbows, blunderbusses, and cannons displays thousands of tin soldiers refighting historic battles on Swiss soil. It will fascinate military-history buffs and children alike. The hall is adorned with a heroic fresco and a cartoon by Ferdinand Hodler (1853–1918), the forceful painter who dominated Swiss art for decades.

Behind the National Museum is a park, known as Platzpromenade and popularly called Platzspitz (tip of the square), on a triangular peninsula formed by the confluence of the Limmat and Sihl rivers. Amid old trees there are a few statues of Swiss celebrities and a music pavilion that was erected for a national exhibition in 1883 (see p. 86).

The National Museum's two outlying branches are the Wohnmuseum (Museum of Dwellings) and the Porcelain and Fayence Collection.

The **Wohnmuseum** is located at 22 Bärengasse (2111716), entrance from Basteiplatz near Paradeplatz. It is open 11 A.M. to noon and 2 to 5 P.M. Monday to Friday;

Sunday, 10 A.M. to noon; and 2 to 4 P.M. Saturday. Admission is free. Contained in two houses from the sixteenth and seventeenth centuries that in 1972 were moved some 180 feet (60 meters) to the present location, the museum shows the interiors of Zurich upper-class homes from 1650 to 1840. A collection of dolls can be seen in the basement.

The Porcelain and Fayence Collection, 20 Münsterhof (2212807), is in the Zunfthaus zur Meisen (p. 54), entrance from the side facing the Fraumünster. The hours are the same as at the Wohnmuseum. Free admission. On display are eighteenth-century ceramics from various Swiss factories.

Kunsthaus, 1 Heimplatz (2516755), on the east bank of the Limmat, is open 10 A.M. to 9 P.M. Tuesday to Friday, and 10 A.M. to 5 P.M. Saturday and Sunday. Admission is $2.15; for periodic special exhibitions, $3.60 to $6.45. Reduced prices for children, students, and groups of more than twenty persons. An entrance for visitors in wheelchairs is on Hirschengraben, at the rear side of the Kunsthaus. A cafeteria is on the premises.

In 1910 Karl Moser designed the nucleus of a building that during the following decades would be substantially enlarged by three additions (the latest in 1976). The works of art on view range from medieval paintings and sculptures to present-day creations.

The visitor is greeted by Hodler frescoes (compare p. 63) and sculptures by Augusto Giacometti. Several showrooms are dedicated to Romanesque and Gothic art, old Italian and Flemish masters, and baroque paintings (Rembrandt, Rubens, Tiepolo, and others).

The main strength of the Kunsthaus is its collection of nineteenth- and twentieth-century art. The Swiss painters

Arnold Böcklin and Hodler (with scores of works) are well represented, as are Augusto Giacometti, his brother Giovanni, and his nephew Alberto, and the creator of weird assemblages and mobiles, Jean Tinguely. In addition, there are important works by Manet, Renoir, Monet, Cézanne, van Gogh, James Ensor, Oskar Kokoschka, Egon Schiele, and Lovis Corinth. Also: a group of paintings by Edvard Munch; a dozen Chagalls; various well-known Picassos; bronzes by Matisse; outstanding paintings by Kandinsky and Klee; plus many works by dadaists (p. 58), surrealists, abstractionists, and artists of other modern schools. A large new section is devoted to American art since World War II, including works by Mark Rothko and Andy Warhol.

Rietberg Museum, Villa Wesendonck, 15 Gablerstrasse (2024528), is in a park (the Rieterpark) in the sloping Rietberg section west of the lake (No. 7 tram). Open 10 A.M. to 5 P.M. Tuesday to Sunday, also 5 to 9 P.M. Wednesday. Admission: $2.15 (children and students, 72¢); Wednesday evening and Sunday, free. Admission for special exhibitions: $4.30, students and children half price. A rich collection of extra-European art can be viewed in a nineteenth-century mansion where Richard Wagner was a house guest and did some writing and composing in 1857–58. The building, in Italianate neoclassical style, was commissioned during the early 1850s by the wealthy German merchant Otto Wesendonck; it is today owned by the city of Zurich.

In 1952 the German banker Baron Eduard von der Heydt donated to Zurich thousands of non-European objects he had gathered over many years. They were transferred into the Villa Wesendonck and form the bulk of a museum that has since been enlarged by other acquisitions.

The exhibits include sculptures, paintings, ceramics, and sundry artifacts produced during various epochs in India, Tibet, China, Japan, Oceania, Africa, and Western Asia, as well as by pre-Colombian American cultures.

The overflow of the Rietberg Museum is on view in the **Villa Schönberg,** 14 Gablergasse, near Villa Wesendonck; same hours of operation. The Rietberg Museum organizes special exhibitions of non-European art at an outlying branch, **Haus zum Kiel,** 20 Hirschengraben (2619652), near the Kunsthaus. Open 2 to 7 P.M. Tuesday to Friday (Thursday until 9 P.M.), 2 to 5 P.M. Saturday, 10 A.M. to 5 P.M. Sunday during shows. Free admission.

Foundation E. G. Bührle Collection, 172 Zollikerstrasse (550086), is on the eastern lakeshore (No. 2 or No. 4 tram to the Wildbachstrasse stop, then walk eastward a few blocks, crossing the rail line). Open 2 to 5 P.M. Tuesday and Friday, 2 to 8 P.M. on the first Friday of each month; during special exhibitions also open 5 to 8 P.M. Wednesday. Admission: $4.70, students $2.15. Housed in a villa, this important private collection rounds out the treasures of the Kunsthaus with significant works by French artists of the nineteenth and twentieth centuries: Delacroix, Courbet, Degas, Manet, Cézanne, Renoir, Matisse, Toulouse-Lautrec, and Gauguin. Furthermore, there are two remarkable van Goghs, paintings by Italian and Dutch masters from the sixteenth century, and a group of medieval religious wood sculptures.

Design Museum (Museum für Gestaltung), 60 Ausstellungsstrasse (2716700), is on the left bank of the Limmat behind the main rail terminal (No. 4 tram). Open 10 A.M. to 6 P.M. Tuesday to Friday (Wednesday until 9 P.M.), 10 A.M. to 5 P.M. Saturday and Sunday. Admission: $2.15, students half price, children free. Formerly the Arts and

Crafts Museum (see next entry), the building contains a school, a large specialized library, 200,000 posters from all over the world, and designs and graphics from the sixteenth century to the present. The museum organizes periodic exhibitions on industrial and urban design, environmental planning, visual communication, and art education.

Bellerive Arts and Crafts Museum, Villa Bellerive, 3 Höschgasse (3834376), is on the eastern lakeshore (No. 2 or No. 4 tram to Höschgasse stop). Open 10 A.M. to 5 P.M. Tuesday to Sunday; during special exhibitions also open 5 to 9 P.M. Wednesday. (Check with the daily press and watch wall posters.) Free admission unless otherwise stated.

Parts of Switzerland's largest arts and crafts collection can be viewed on a rotating basis in periodic exhibitions. (Because of space limitations, most of it remains in storage.) The museum, in a villa built during the early 1930s, is noteworthy above all for its wealth of objects representing the Jugendstil (the German name for art nouveau): furniture, textiles, ceramics, and glassware. There are also items from non-European areas, jewelry, and many examples of fashion and industrial design in the twentieth century up to the present.

Heidi Weber Private Museum, the last building by the Swiss architect Le Corbusier (Charles-Édouard Jeanneret), 8 Höschgasse (3836470), is near the Villa Bellerive (see preceding entry). Open 2 to 8 P.M. Wednesday and 2 to 5 P.M. Thursday to Sunday from the middle of May to the end of September. Admission: $5.70, students $3.60. The influential Le Corbusier, who suggested plans for the Palace of the League of Nations in Geneva and contributed designs for United Nations headquarters in New York, was still working on this structure near the Lake of Zurich when he died in 1965. The house, in a garden, is a composition of concrete, steel, glass, and color panels; it contains sculpture, paintings, and textiles designed by Le Corbusier.

Graphics Collection, 101 Rämistrasse, entrance from Künstlergasse (2564046), is in the Federal Polytechnic College. Open 10 A.M. to 5 P.M. Monday to Friday; during special exhibitions also open 1 to 5 P.M. Saturday. Free admission. A large collection of woodcuts, engravings, etchings, and prints by masters from Dürer, Rembrandt, Canaletto, and Piranesi to Munch and Picasso.

Archeological Collection, 73 Rämistrasse (2572820), is in the university building. Open 1 to 6 P.M. Tuesday to Friday. Free admission. Sumerian, Assyrian, and Persian sculptures and reliefs; an Egyptian mummy and Egyptian art; Minoan, Greek, Etruscan, and Roman pottery and bronzes; and plaster casts of seven hundred ancient sculptures.

Ethnological Museum of the Zurich University, 40 Pelikanstrasse (2213191), is in the former Botanical Garden (No. 2 or No. 9 tram to Sihlstrasse stop). Open 10 A.M. to 1 P.M. and 2 to 8 P.M. Wednesday, 10 A.M. to 1 P.M. and 2 to 5 P.M. Thursday and Friday, 11 A.M. to 5 P.M. Saturday and Sunday. Free admission. A collection of twenty-five thousand objects from non-European cultures illustrating their history, religions, art, handicrafts, and folklore. Also exhibits focusing on present-day conditions in developing societies. Periodic exhibitions on special themes.

Other Zurich University collections open to the general public (free admission):

Anthropological Museum, 190 Winterthurerstrasse (2575411), is on the northwestern outskirts of the city (No.

9 or No. 10 tram to the last stop). Open 9 A.M. to 5 P.M. Tuesday to Friday.

Paleontological Museum, 16 Künstlergasse (2572339), is in the main building of the university. Open 9 A.M. to 5 P.M. Tuesday to Friday, 10 A.M. to 4 P.M. Saturday and Sunday.

Medical History Collection, 16 Künstlergasse (2572298), is in the university building. Open 1 to 6 P.M. Tuesday to Friday, 11 A.M. to 5 P.M. Saturday and Sunday. Medical equipment, literature, and documents from various epochs; reconstructions of a pharmacy, circa 1750, and of a delivery room, circa 1850.

Zoological Museum, 16 Künstlergasse (2573821), is in the university building. Open 9 A.M. to 5 P.M. Tuesday to Friday, 10 A.M. to 4 P.M. Saturday and Sunday. Skeletons of large Ice Age animals; various animals from Switzerland and other countries. Visitors may watch insects or small live aquatic fauna through microscopes, listen to the recorded sounds of birds and other animals, and select other audiovisual demonstrations.

Geological and Mineralogical Collection, 5 Sonneggstrasse, E Floor (2562211), is part of the Federal Polytechnic College. Open 10 A.M. to 7 P.M. Monday to Friday, 10 A.M. to 4 P.M. Saturday. Free admission. On display are fossils, rocks, minerals, reliefs, and geological maps.

Museum of the North American Indian (Indianermuseum), 89 Feldstrasse (2410050), is in the workers' district of Aussersihl, west of the main rail terminal (No. 31 bus from Hauptbahnhof to Hohlstrasse stop). Open 2 to 5 P.M. Saturday, 10 A.M. to noon Sunday. Free admission. Housed in a school building, this museum claims to be western Europe's sole major collection devoted to the cultures of Native Americans. Fourteen hundred exhibits include tepees, clothing, blankets, ornaments, masks, and cult objects. The illustrated catalog costs $22.

Thomas Mann Archives, 15 Schönberggasse, third floor (2564045), is near the university. Open 2 to 4 P.M. Wednesday and Saturday or by telephone appointment. Free admission. The study and library of the Nobel laureate, with many manuscripts and documents, were transferred after his death in 1955 from his last home in a villa in the western lakeshore suburb of Kilchberg to the present location, a seventeenth-century house where Goethe once stayed. The archives, owned by the Federal Polytechnic College, also include literature about Thomas Mann. (For Mann's grave, see p. 77.)

Toy Museum, 15 Fortunagasse, 6th floor (2119305), is off Rennweg in the city center. Take the elevator (no access for wheelchair users). Open 2 to 5 P.M. Monday to Friday, 1 to 4 P.M. Sunday. Free admission. This collection of European toys from the end of the eighteenth century to the beginning of the twentieth century was assembled by the owners of the toy firm Franz Carl Weber (main shop is at 43 Rennweg). There are quaint old dolls and dollhouses, steam-engine models, toy trains, and other mechanical delights for children and nostalgic adults, as well as children's books and games.

Museum of Tin Figures, 19 Obere Zäune (2625720), is near Grossmünster. Open 2 to 4 P.M. Tuesday to Friday, 2 to 5 P.M. Saturday, 10 A.M. to noon and 1 to 4 P.M. Sunday. No access for wheelchair users. Admission: $2.90, children half price. Located in a picturesque house that dates back to the thirteenth century and was enlarged during the Renaissance, this collection in four rooms contains toys and historical figurines made of pewter, once a Swiss industry.

Jacobs Suchard Museum, Collection of the Cultural History of Coffee, 17 Seefeldquai (3835651), is on the eastern lakeshore (No. 2 or No. 4 tram to Feldeggstrasse stop, then walk toward the lake). Open 2 to 5 P.M. Friday and Saturday, 10 A.M. to 5 P.M. Sunday. (Closed between Christmas and New Year.) No access for wheelchair users. Free admission. The museum, organized by a Swiss coffee-importing and chocolate firm, claims to be unique. It contains silverware, porcelain, graphics, and paintings connected with coffee, and a library with two thousand titles on the subject.

Beyer Museum of Time Measurement, 31 Bahnhofstrasse (2211080), is centrally located. Open 10 A.M. to noon and 2 to 4 P.M. Monday to Friday. No access for wheelchair users. Free admission. Located above the watch and jewelry store of the old firm Beyer Chronometrie, the collection shows how time was measured in antiquity and displays timepieces, including grandfather clocks, from the sixteenth century to the present.

Kulturama, 60 Espenhofweg (4932525), is on the western outskirts (No. 14 tram to the last stop in the Triemli section, then walk north to the Letzi school complex). Open 10 A.M. to 5 P.M. Monday to Friday and on the first Sunday of each month. Admission: $3.58, students and children $2.15. The exhibits trace the evolution of plant, animal, and human life over millions of years. On display are fossils, bones, skulls, tools (originals and reconstructions); also charts mapping the history of medicine; graphics, photographs, models, and specimens demonstrating human development from conception to birth; birth control methods.

Mühlerama (Mill Museum), 231 Seefeldstrasse (557660), is on the western lakeshore (No. 2 or No. 4 tram to the last stop). Open 2 to 5 P.M. Tuesday to Saturday, 1:30 to 6 P.M. Sunday. No access for wheelchair users. Admission: $3.58, children $2.15. The museum is a functioning mill, installed in 1913 in a one-hundred-year-old building that originally was a brewery. The flour mill ceased commercial operations in 1983. What is being shown now on four levels is the processing of grain to flour, as well as exhibits about the growing and trading of cereals, the milling industry, food surpluses, and hunger in the world. Fresh bread is sold on the premises on Friday.

The thoroughly restored rambling brick building of the old brewery also houses a trendy restaurant and piano bar, **Blaue Ente** (Blue Duck), with entrance at 223 Seefeldstrasse (557706), open from noon to 11 P.M. daily. Lunch or dinner, with some wine, costs around $35 a person. A wine shop, **Vinothek Bacchus,** is in the same building, 225 Seefeldstrasse (554522). Located in the same complex are a commercial modern-art gallery, **Turske & Turske,** 225 Seefeldstrasse (559770), a ballet school, a music studio, and private apartments.

Temporary exhibitions are frequently held in various locations around the city. Following are the most noteworthy sites:

Stadthaus, 17 Stadthausquai (2163111), adjoins the Fraumünster. Open 9 A.M. to 6 P.M. Monday to Friday. Free admission. Exhibits in the corridors of this municipal building, which contains offices and archives, feature various topics that pertain to Zurich.

Strauhof, 9 Augustinerstrasse (2163139), off Bahnhofstrasse, is centrally located. Open 10 A.M. to 6 P.M. Tuesday
to Sunday, also 6 to 9 P.M. Thursday. Free admission.

The massive building from the seventeenth century,
now city-owned, on a picturesquely curving and sloping
street, was restored in the late 1980s. Changing exhibitions
are held in the stuccoed rooms on the ground and second
floors. The top floor is taken up by the **James Joyce Archives** (2118301). The four showrooms and workrooms,
including a library with three thousand volumes of Joyci-
ana, are open 2 to 6 P.M. Tuesday to Thursday and can be
visited at other times if you phone for an appointment. No
access for wheelchair users.

James Joyce and his family lived in Zurich during
World War I and again during World War II until the Irish
writer's death in 1941. (Compare p. 44, James Joyce Pub,
and p. 77, Fluntern Cemetery.)

Haus zum Rech, 4 Neumarkt (2622081), is northwest of
the Kunsthaus. Open 8 A.M. to 6 P.M. Monday to Friday,
8 to 11:30 A.M. Saturday. Free admission. No access for
wheelchair users. The outwardly sober building goes back
to the Middle Ages and was the residence of several Zurich
mayors. The narrow courtyard is remarkable for its Italian
Renaissance architecture, rococo ironwork banisters, and
frescoed landings. The well-restored edifice is the seat of
the city's architectural archives, contains a large model of
Zurich from around 1800 and a collection of city views,
and serves for periodic exhibitions on the city's archeology
and architectural history.

Helmhaus, 31 Limmatquai (2516177), is next to the Wasserkirche. Open 10 A.M. to 6 P.M. Tuesday to Sunday,
also 6 to 9 P.M. Thursday. Free admission. A bridge once
traversed the open ground-floor hall of this building, link-

ing the island on which it and the Wasserkirche rose with either bank of the Limmat. Court hearings were held and linen cloth was traded in the wooden structure. The present edifice, in neoclassical style, was built at the end of the eighteenth century. Swiss contemporary art is the main theme of the periodic exhibitions in the Helmhaus.

Kunsthalle Zurich, 114 Hardturmstrasse (2721515), is in the industrial section on the west bank of the Limmat (No. 4 tram to the Förrlibuck-Strasse stop). Open noon to 6 P.M. Tuesday to Friday, 11 A.M. to 5 P.M. Saturday and Sunday. Admission: $2.86, students half price. No access for wheelchair users. Operated by a private association, this structure provides austere exhibition space for contemporary artists.

Shedhalle, 395 Seestrasse (4815950), is on the western lakeshore (No. 7 tram to Post Wollishofen stop). Open 2 to 8 P.M. Tuesday to Friday, 2 to 5 P.M. Saturday and Sunday. Free admission. Periodic shows by young artists; plus works of artistic experimentation.

Foundation for Constructivist and Concrete Art, 317 Seefeldstrasse (533808), is on the eastern lakeshore (No. 2 or No. 4 tram to the last stop, Tiefenbrunnen). Open 2 to 5 P.M. Tuesday to Friday, 10 A.M. to 5 P.M. Saturday and Sunday, and at other times on request by phone. Admission: $2.86, students $2.15. Shows by workshops and individual artists of the constructivist movement. Also *Rockefeller Dining Room* model by Fritz Glarner.

Random Sights and Strolls

Zurichers are proud of their parks and lakeshore promenades with lovingly tended flower beds and greenery. If some trees are to be felled in a development project, vocal environmental advocates will try to save them and often succeed—sometimes after a debate in the city Parliament. To the visitor, the neat city with its panorama of the lake and the Alps offers inviting stretches for strolling or otherwise enjoying the outdoors.

Start from the lake end of Bahnhofstrasse and the park at Bürkliplatz and walk along the western lakeshore, General-Guisan-Quai, for about half a mile (800 meters) to a grove, almost at water level, with many exotic trees. An art nouveau fountain marks the entrance to the **Arboretum;** there are also statues and an aviary.

Proceed farther south past bathing establishments, a small harbor, and marinas to reach the **Municipal Collection of Succulent Plants** (Sukkulentensammlung, 88 Mythenquai; 2014554). By tram, take the No. 7 to the Brunaustrasse stop. Open 9 to 11:30 A.M. and 1:30 to 4:30 P.M. daily. Free admission. More than twenty-five thousand cactuses, aloes, and other fleshy plants from various continents can be viewed in the greenhouses.

Other attractive public gardens in the area are the **Belvoirpark** at the west side of Mythenquai and Alfred-Escher-Strasse, and above it, across the long Seestrasse, the **Rieterpark** (p. 65).

The Botanical Gardens, 107 Zollikerstrasse (3854411), are located on the eastern side of the lake (No. 2 or No. 4 tram to the Höschgasse stop; walk eastward). Open 7 A.M. to 7 P.M. Monday to Friday, 8 A.M. to 6 P.M. Saturday and Sunday, March to September; 8 A.M. to 6 P.M. Monday to Friday, 8 A.M. to 5 P.M. Saturday and Sunday, October to February. The greenhouses are open 9:30 to 11:30 A.M. and 1 to 4 P.M. daily. Free admission. Cafeteria.

The vast, rolling terrain, designed according to scientific criteria and tended by Zurich University, is a restful park with benches and chairs. It includes meadows and a patch with trees indigenous to Switzerland; displays of food plants, kitchen herbs and medicinal plants; and three translucent geodesic domes over vegetation from tropical rain forests, subtropical areas, and savannas. A printed guide can be bought at the cafeteria for $7.15.

At the lakefront, not quite half a mile (600 meters) down from the Botanical Gardens on the **Zurichhorn** peninsula is another extensive park. (For lake boats that make stops here, see pp. 30–31.) Statues of Swiss notables, sculptures by modern artists, and a large mobile assemblage by Jean Tinguely (1964) adorn this vast recreation area. There are also a bathing beach and a warm-weather restaurant with a terrace overlooking the lake and a straw-thatched bungalow, **Fischstube Zürichhorn,** 160 Bellerivestrasse (552520). Freshwater and sea fish are conspicuous on the menu, but there are other dishes as well. Lunch with beverage runs $35 to $40 a person. Nearby, at 170 Bellerivestrasse, is the **Casino Zürichhorn** (552020), a convention and banquet center with its own restaurant.

A stroll in the Zurichhorn park can be combined with visits to the **Bellerive Arts and Crafts Museum** and the **Heidi Weber Private Museum** (pp. 67–68).

The **Old Botanical Gardens,** on the Schanzengraben canal west of Bahnhofstrasse, is now a public park with the **Ethnological Museum** (p. 68).

Officially called Zoologischer Garten Zurich, the **Zoo** is located at 221 Zürichbergstrasse (for recorded information, call 2527100; for offices, 2515411) on the Zürichberg (take the No. 6 tram to last stop). Open 8 A.M. to 6 P.M. daily. Admission: $5.50, students $2.75, children $2.36. Reduced rates for groups of more than twenty persons.

Restaurant. Opened in 1929, Zurich's zoo houses more than 1,500 animals belonging to some 250 different species, including an Asian elephant family and snow leopards. A recently built structure contains a rain forest hall, aviary, aquarium, and vivarium.

Joyceans will want to visit the grave of the Irish writer (compare p. 73) in the **Fluntern cemetery** at 189 Zürich-bergstrasse, close to the zoo. Open 7 A.M. (November to February, 8 A.M.) until sunset. Take the first cemetery entrance near the Zoo tram stop, walk up an alley of birches all the way, then turn right; steps on your left lead to the grave, marked with a statue of Joyce. The life-size bronze by the American sculptor Milton Hebald (1966) is a likeness of the writer in his mature years, eyeglasses and all, seated on a square stone with his legs crossed, an open book in his right hand.

Joyce's wife, Nora, who stayed in Zurich after his death in 1941 and died in the city in 1951, and their son, Giorgio, who died in Germany in 1976, are also buried here.

Following are the resting places of some other prominent figures in and around Zurich: **Thomas Mann** (1875–1955; p. 70) is buried in Kilchberg Cemetery, in a suburb on the west side of the lake (No. 161 bus from Bürkliplatz at the lake end of Bahnhofstrasse.) The ashes of **Jean-Henri Dunant,** cofounder of the International Red Cross and winner of the Nobel Peace Prize (1828–1910), are at Sihlfeld Crematorium, Albisrieders-trasse (No. 3 tram), on the western outskirts. **Gottfried Keller,** the Swiss novelist and poet (1819–90), is buried in the cemetery in the Sihlfeld complex. To see the grave of **Carl Gustav Jung,** the psychologist and psychiatrist (1875–1961), pay a visit to Küsnacht Cemetery (No. 916 bus from Bellevue-Platz, or S-7 train). Visit the grave of **Otto Klemperer,** conductor (1885–1973), at the Jewish

Cemetery, 330 Friesenberg-Strasse on the western outskirts (No. 14 tram from Hauptbahnhof to Goldbrunner
Platz and No. 32 bus).

BEYOND SIGHTSEEING

Music in Zurich

The season in the **Opera House** (p. 60) runs from the end
of September to the first week of July, reaching its climax
during the Zurich June Festival. The institution offers
grand opera, an occasional operetta, ballet, concerts by its
own orchestra, and recitals by international stars.

The Zurich Opera is recognized as belonging to the top
tier of the lyric theater, along with Milan's La Scala, the
opera houses of Vienna, Munich, and a few other European
cities, and New York's Metropolitan Opera.

For many performances virtually all seats are reserved
for subscribers, but there is always a chance that one or the
other ticket becomes available. Inquire about nonsubscription performances and order seats at Billetkasse, Opernhaus Zurich, 1 Falkenstrasse, CH-8008 Zurich (2529307).
Requests for opera tickets are also handled by the Zurich
Tourist Office, 15 Bahnhofplatz, CH-8023 Zurich
(2110505, fax 2113981).

Ticket prices range from about $15 for the cheapest
gallery seats at an ordinary opera performance to close to
$300 for a dress-circle seat at a gala premiere. Seats for
concerts and recitals cost $6 to $48. Sales of nonsubscription tickets that have not been reserved earlier start one
month before the day of performance. The Opera House
box office (Billetkasse, 2620909) is open 10 A.M. to 7 P.M.
Monday to Saturday.

Concerts and recitals are held in the **Tonhalle** (p. 59) on many days from September to the end of June. The Tonhalle Orchestra, founded in 1868, is Switzerland's oldest symphony group; it has performed at Carnegie Hall in New York, in Japan, and in other countries. Guest orchestras, chamber music groups, virtuosos, and singers are often heard at the Tonhalle. Ticket prices range from $8 to $70. Requests for tickets to nonsubscription events are to be mailed well ahead of the day of performance to Billetkasse, Tonhalle-Gesellschaft, 5 Gotthardstrasse, CH-8002 Zurich (fax 2012364). Sales of nonsubscription tickets that have not been reserved by mail start at the Tonhalle box office, 7 Claridenstrasse (2111580), one month before the day of performance. The box office is open 10 A.M. to 6 P.M. Monday to Friday, and 10 A.M. to noon Saturday.

Concerts by various groups or soloists—not exclusively sacred music—are held often in the **Grossmünster** (p. 56), the **Fraumünster** (p. 54), and other churches. Occasional concerts or recitals take place also at the **Konservatorium** (Conservatory), 6 Florhofgasse (2518955), near the Kunsthaus. For music programs, consult *What's On*, a brochure published periodically by the Zurich Tourist Office, the daily press, and the wall posters "Concerts in Zurich."

An **International Jazz Festival** is held from the end of October to the beginning of November every year at the Volkshaus, 60 Stauffacherstrasse (2416404), a headquarters of labor organizations, in the workers' district west of the main rail terminal (No. 2 and No. 3 trams).

Good jazz can often be heard at **Widder Bar,** 6 Widdergasse (2113150), at the southern end of Rennweg, in several places in the Niederdorf section, and at **Kaufleuten Restaurant,** 18 Pelikanstrasse (2211505), in the city center.

Pop and rock concerts take place frequently at **Hallen-stadion,** 45 Wallisellen-Strasse (3113030), a sports hall in the Oerlikon section on the northeastern outskirts (several S-Bahn lines run from Hauptbahnhof to Oerlikon station). Consult *What's On* and the local dailies.

Theater

Zurich's principal stage for legitimate drama in standard German is the **Schauspielhaus** (p. 61), 34 Rämistrasse (2511111; program information, 2022222). The box office is open 10 A.M. to 7 P.M. Monday to Saturday and 10 A.M. to noon Sunday. Tickets to the day's performance can be bought until curtain time.

Schauspielhaus Keller (2655858; program information, 2655760), the basement stage of the Schauspielhaus, produces contemporary and experimental plays for audiences of up to five hundred.

Smaller theaters:

Theater am Neumarkt, 5 Neumarkt (box office, 2514488), near Spiegelgasse, 300 seats; mostly modern drama. **Theater am Hechtplatz,** 7 Hechtplatz (2523234), 260 seats; vaudeville, cabaret. **Bernhard Theater,** Theaterplatz (2526055), 450 seats at tables in the Opera House annex; musicals, cabaret, farces. **Theater 11,** 7 Thurgauerstrasse (3113444), in the modern Stadthof 11 complex in the Oerlikon section near Hallenstadion, 900 seats; frequent appearances of Italian and other non–German-speaking troupes.

Puppentheater Sonnenhof, 12 Stadelhofer-Strasse (2529424), near the Opera House. Puppetry for children and adults: Grimm fairy tales, Pinocchio, and the like, often in Zurich dialect.

Rote Fabrik, 395 Seestrasse (4819143; box office,
4824212), a former industrial plant on the western lakeshore in the Wollishofen suburb (No. 161 or 165 bus from
Bürkliplatz at the lake end of Bahnhofstrasse). Since the
radical youth riots of 1980, the nearly one-hundred-year-
old "red factory" functions as an alternative cultural center;
it occasionally produces avant-garde plays.

For programs and for other small and experimental
stages, watch Zurich's daily press.

Tickets for the Opera House, for concerts, and for
most theaters can also be bought at Billettzentrale (Ticket
Center) of the Zurich Tourist Office, Werdmühleplatz
(2212283) off Uraniastrasse between Bahnhofstrasse and
the Limmat, and often at one of the department stores.

Cinema

Zurich has two dozen major movie houses. Consult the local
newspapers for their programs. Films are usually screened in
their original language with or without subtitles.

Night Life

The nearly forty night spots in Zurich ordinarily close at
2 A.M., but some are permitted to stay open until 4 A.M.
the next morning on Saturday and Sunday. Prices for
drinks and food generally go up after midnight. Under
local regulations, nonalcoholic drinks must be available at
all times.

In addition to the boîtes in some hotels (pp. 31 and
following), late-night cafés, bars, and discotheques will be
found particularly in the Niederdorf section and in other
central neighborhoods. Among them: **Limmatbar,** 82

Limmatquai (2616530); **Joker Dancing,** 5 Gotthardstrasse
(2022262), in the Kongresshaus, with floor shows; **King
Club,** 25 Talstrasse (2112333), near Paradeplatz, floor
shows. For others, watch for publicity in local dailies.

Folklore

Zurichers may have a reputation for staidness, but some of
them do a little frolic at carnival time. The local **Fasnacht**
(carnival) is observed with a downtown parade on the
Thursday after Ash Wednesday. Before and after that day
small bands of musicians drift from one tavern to the other,
especially on the east bank of the Limmat, to play harsh-
sounding tunes.

The memory of the medieval craftsmen's and merchants' guilds (compare p. 42) is revived annually by rous-
ing parades in celebration of spring. These parades take
place in the Bahnhofstrasse and the surrounding neighborhood on the afternoon of the third Monday in April.
Known as the **Sechseläuten** (in Zurich dialect, Sächse-
lüte), the festivities include the ringing of church bells at
6 P.M., a sound that once signaled the end of the working day. Actually, on Sechseläuten day many stores now
close at 2 P.M. and most office workers have the afternoon
off.

The people in historic costumes who march down
Bahnhofstrasse behind brass bands aren't really carpenters
or hatters as the old names of their associations would
indicate, but computer analysts, bank tellers, and municipal officials. The guilds to which they belong are in fact
social clubs and old-boy networks.

The spring festivities climax in the burning of a man-
size straw puppet, called the Böög and symbolizing winter,
on a pyre in Sechseläuten-Platz between Bellevue-Platz and

the Opera House. A torch is put to the heap of flammable material at 6 P.M. sharp as thousands of people—the participants in the earlier guild parades and many young people—stand around and watch. A big cheer goes up when the flames eventually lick at the Böög and the straw puppet writhes, topples, and is consumed by fire. The rite is ominously remindful of how medieval criminals and heretics died at the stake. Zurichers consider it a good omen if the straw puppet burns quickly, and some people take bets on the number of minutes the Böög resists.

Sechseläuten is preceded by a children's parade in the city center on the Sunday before the third Monday in April.

Every three years or so the northern bay of Lake Zurich, reaching into the city center, becomes an outdoor stage for a **weekend festival** in June or July that culminates in a huge display of fireworks. On the lakefront street vendors sell sausages and sweets, sidewalk mimes perform, and a ferris wheel and various rides do business in Theaterplatz near the Opera House.

During the second weekend in September a three-day outdoor fair surrounds the oldest of Zurich's popular observances, **Knabenschiessen** (Boys' Shooting Contest). In an ancient rite of preparation for service in the citizens' militia, boys between the ages of twelve and sixteen prove their marksmanship and compete for prizes. The contest takes place at the municipal shooting range, a walled complex at 341 Uetlibergstrasse at the foot of the Uetliberg on the southwestern outskirts. For information on the fair, consult the local dailies.

Exercise

Jogging. The promenades and parks on either shore of Lake Zurich are most convenient for jogging. Walkers and joggers who prefer to work out on forest paths take the No. 6 tram to the last stop on the Zürichberg, Fluntern section, or the S-10 up the Uetliberg.

Swimming. Several bathing establishments are on the east and west shores of Lake Zurich. The Municipal Beach at 95 Mythenquai (2010000), near Belvoirpark, also houses a restaurant. A large private pool with artificial waves is at 36 Adlisberg-Strasse (2617102), near the Dolder Grand Hotel. For other open-air and indoor pools, see the Zurich telephone directory under *Schwimmbäder*.

Tennis. Courts can be rented by the hour at ten municipal sports facilities in various parts of the city, for instance, at 200 Mythenquai (2023243) on the western lakeshore. Consult the Zurich telephone directory under *Sportamt der Stadt Zürich—Tennisanlagen*. Several private tennis clubs also admit guests; see the telephone directory under *Tennisanlagen* and *Tennisclubs*. For professional trainers, make arrangements by phone or on the spot when renting a tennis court.

Bicycling. Bicycles can be rented at Zurich's main rail terminal (Hauptbahnhof, 2453477) and suburban railroad stations. Rentals for four to twenty-four hours are $4 to $10. Bicycling lanes are marked along the lakeshores.

Golf. The golf courses closest to Zurich are Dolder Golf Club (2515535), near the Dolder Grand Hotel, and the Golf und Country Club Zurich, Zumikon (9180050). Both are for members only but will provide information on where visitors may play.

Horseback Riding. For riding schools and clubs, see the Zurich telephone directory under *Reitschulen und -anstalten*.

Skiing. The runs closest to Zurich, with several ski lifts,

are on the 6,086-foot (1,855-meter) Hoch-Ybrig Mountain, about 20 miles (32 kilometers) southeast of the city.
It takes an hour to reach the mountain: ride the railroad to
the ancient abbey town of Einsiedeln and then proceed by
bus and cableway. The winter sports center of St. Moritz
is a four-hour rail trip away.

Ice-skating. Zurich's skating rinks, with artificial ice, are
open from October to March. Municipal rinks are at 71
Wasserschöpfi (4629822), at the foot of the Uetliberg (No.
14 tram), and at 80 Siewerdtstrasse (3124090), in the Oerlikon section on the northeastern outskirts (several S-Bahn
lines run from Hauptbahnhof to Oerlikon station). A private ice-skating rink is at 36 Adlisberg-Strasse (2617102),
near the Dolder Grand Hotel.

Spectator Sports

Soccer. Matches of the Swiss national championship
and international games are played at the stadium of the
Grasshopper-Club Zurich, Hardturm-Strasse, in the industrial district on the left bank of the Limmat (No. 4 tram
to the last stop). Tickets, 321 Hardturm-Strasse (2723388).
Also other soccer games at Letzigrund Stadium of Fussball-
Club Zürich, Letzigraben, in the Outersihl section west of
Hauptbahnhof (No. 2 tram). Tickets (only on playing
days) at Billetkasse, 47 Herdernstrasse (4929560).

An international **track-and-field** meet takes place in
the Letzigrund Stadium in August. For information, call
4927474 or consult the Zurich press.

Ice hockey events are held in the Hallenstadion, 73
Wallisellen-Strasse (3113030), in the Oerlikon section. **Bi-
cycle races** also take place in the Hallenstadion. Watch for
announcements in the local dailies.

Emergencies

Few uniformed police personnel are seen on Zurich's streets as a rule, but the city is nevertheless well policed by municipal and cantonal officers. The **police emergency number** is 117. For nonemergency calls, contact either of the two law enforcement organizations operating in Zurich: city police, 2167111; cantonal police, 2472211.

Zurich has long had a reputation for being, to a vast extent, free of street crime. This has changed since the beginning of the 1980s. Many residents have blamed the continued influx of poor foreigners and the relatively high number of drug addicts for the recent increase in thefts, robberies, and assaults. In the late 1980s Platzspitz park became the locale of a social experiment under city auspices whereby the use and sale of small quantities of hard drugs in the area was tolerated and warm food and clean syringes were dispensed. At one time as many as three thousand drug addicts from all over Switzerland and from neighboring countries were crowding the Platzspitz. Most Zurichers shunned the park. There were deaths from narcotics overdoses, and street crime spilled into nearby neighborhoods. In 1991 the authorities conceded failure of the attempt at liberalizing drug use and ghettoizing addicts. Platzspitz was closed at night, and police patrolled the park around the clock. The area around the main rail terminal (Hauptbahnhof) was considered at risk, particularly after dark, and the authorities decided in 1992 to close the Platzspitz park and the Shopville underground mall at night. Compared with the situation in quite a few other Western cities, the streets of Zurich are nevertheless enviably safe at any hour.

The **fire department emergency number** is 118.

In case of **medical emergency,** call 144 or 3616161 for

an ambulance. The University Hospital, 100 Rämistrasse (2551111), operates a twenty-four-hour emergency ward.

Zurich's medical establishment is vast and internationally renowned. In addition to the University Hospital (also known as Cantonal Hospital) with its many specialized departments and clinics, there is an array of other public and private medical institutions. Consult the Zurich telephone directory under *Spitäler*. Doctors are listed by specialty under *Aerzte*. Many physicians speak English.

Services

Post offices provide regular services 7:30 A.M. to 6:30 P.M. Monday to Friday, and 7:30 to 11 A.M. Saturday. The central post office, Sihlpost, 95–99 Kasernenstrasse (2454111), on the Sihl embankment near the main rail terminal, handles urgent matters at a special window *(Dringlichkeitsschalter)*, charging higher rates, 6:30 to 10:30 P.M. Monday to Friday, 6:30 A.M. to 8 P.M. Saturday, and 11 A.M. to 10:30 P.M. Sunday.

Banks are generally open 8:15 A.M. to 4:30 P.M. Monday to Friday (until 6 P.M. on Thursday). Some bank branches in the city center have longer office hours and also do business on Saturday morning. Currency exchanges at Kloten Airport and at the main rail terminal are open 6:45 A.M. to 10:45 P.M. daily.

City offices are usually open 8:30 A.M. to 4:30 P.M. (Thursday until 6 P.M.); **cantonal offices,** 8 to 11:45 A.M. and 1:30 to 5 P.M. Monday to Friday.

Following are various services that a visitor may require:

Alcoholics Anonymous. Contact the AA Service Office at 7 Cramerstrasse (2413030), west of the Sihl River (No.

2 or No. 3 tram to Stauffacher Platz). The emergency phone is staffed until midnight daily.

Babysitters. Kady Service, 6 Pfalzgasse (2113786), is near Rennweg in the city center. The Globus and Jelmoli department stores (see next section) take care of children during business hours.

Consulates. The United States Consulate General is located at 141 Zollikerstrasse (552566), east of the lake (No. 912 bus from the Bellevue-Plaz). Office hours are 9 A.M. to 12:30 P.M. Monday to Friday, and 2 to 4 P.M. Monday to Wednesday and Friday. British Consular Services are at 56 Dufour Strasse (471520), on the eastern lakeshore (No. 2 or No. 4 tram). Office hours are 9 A.M. to noon and 2 to 4 P.M. Monday to Friday. For Canadian Consular Services, contact the Canadian Embassy in Bern, 88 Kirchenfeld-Strasse (031-446381).

Dentists. A listing of dentists is in the Zurich telephone directory under *Zahnärzte.*

Lawyers. Look under *Rechtsanwälte* in the telephone directory.

Library. Zentralbibliothek, 6 Zähringerplatz (2617272) in the Niederdorf section, is a combined cantonal, municipal, and academic institution. Its reading rooms are open 8 A.M. to 8 P.M. Monday to Friday, and 8 A.M. to 5 P.M. Saturday. The reference shelves also house English-language volumes.

Lost property. For objects lost anywhere in the city and on public transport, except on railroad trains and in the main rail terminal, inquire at Fundbüro, 10 Werdmühle-strasse (2162550), in the office complex near Hauptbahnhof and Bahnhofstrasse. Open 7:30 A.M. to 5:30 P.M. Monday to Friday. On Saturday and Sunday, inquire at the police station, 3 Bahnhofquai (2167111), near Hauptbahnhof. The phone number for the lost property office at the main rail terminal is 2118811.

Pharmacies. See the listing in the Zurich telephone directory under *Apotheken*. A twenty-four-hour pharmacy is the Bellevue Apotheke, 14 Theaterstrasse (2524411), near the Opera House.

Religious services. Worshipers can choose from a variety of churches and synagogues.

Protestant services in English: These are held at St. Andrew's Anglican-Episcopal Church, 9 Promenadengasse (2526024), near Bellevue-Platz, 10:30 A.M. Sunday; and, for Evangelical-Reformed, at 10 Schanzengasse, near Bellevue-Platz, 10 A.M. Sunday.

Roman Catholic: Masses in German are held at Liebfrauen Kirche, 34 Weinberg-Strasse (2527474), near Central square, 6:45, 8:30 A.M. and 6:15 P.M. Monday to Friday, 8:30 A.M. and 5:30 P.M. Saturday, 9:30, 11:30 A.M. and 4 and 8 P.M. Sunday. Spanish-language mass is held at 4 Rotwandstrasse (2416650), west of the Sihl River, 6 P.M. Saturday. For English-language masses and devotions, inquire at English Catholic Mission, 52 Im Glockenacker (556485), on the southeastern outskirts.

Synagogues: The Orthodox synagogue at 10 Löwenstrasse (2213892), west of Bahnhofstrasse, dates back to 1884 and was recently restored; the Orthodox temple at 37 Freigutstrasse (2014998), west of the lake and Bahnhofstrasse, was built in 1924. The Rabbinate and Jewish Community (Israelitische Cultusgemeinde), 33 Lavaterstrasse (2011659), is in the Enge section west of the lake.

Tourist information. Official Tourist Office, 15 Bahnhofplatz, CH-8001 Zurich (2114000, fax 2120141), is on
the south side of Hauptbahnhof. It is open 8 A.M. to 10
P.M. Monday to Friday, and 8 A.M. to 8:30 P.M. Saturday
and Sunday, March to October. From November to February, it is open 8 A.M. to 8 P.M. Monday to Thursday, 8
A.M. to 10 P.M. Friday, and 9 A.M. to 6 P.M. Saturday and
Sunday. Branches of the Zurich Tourist Office at Kloten
Airport, Terminals A and B, are open 7 A.M. to 8 P.M.
every day of the year.

Public toilets. Toilets are to be found in the main rail
terminal and suburban railroad stations and in some
squares such as Paradeplatz Bürklipatz at the lake end of
Bahnhofstrasse, and Heimplatz.

Travel services. Travel agents are listed in the Zurich
telephone directory under *Reisebüros*. For airline and air
charter services, see the telephone directory under *Flug-
gesellschaften* and *Flughafen*.

Shopping

Zurich is a consumer's dream, and the Bahnhofstrasse one
of the world's great shopping boulevards. The city's most
elegant stores are on or near that street and around Paradeplatz. The large **department stores** cluster on and off
the northern part of Bahnhofstrasse: Globus, Löwenplatz
and 11 Schweizergasse (2213311); Jelmoli, 1 Seidengasse
(2204411); St. Annahof, 57 Bahnhofstrasse (2211830); and
Vilan, 75 Bahnhofstrasse (2295111). Store hours are 9 A.M.
to 6:30 P.M. Monday to Friday, and 8 A.M. to 4 P.M. Saturday. Many stores stay open until 9 P.M. on Thursday.

  Watch and jewelry shops are conspicuous along
Bahnhofstrasse. The collection of timepieces from all the

famous Swiss firms, diamonds and other gems, and platinum, gold, and silver objects is dazzling.

Also prominent on and around the boulevard are **fashion stores** in which French, Italian, British, and Swiss labels abound. Grieder, 30 Bahnhofstrasse (2113360), is to Zurich what Bloomingdale's is to New York as far as women's and men's luxury fashions are concerned. Swiss-made Bally shoes can be bought in two shops at 32 and 66 Bahnhofstrasse.

Fur and leatherware stores dot the neighborhood as well. Schweizer Heimatwerk, 2 Bahnhofstrasse (2210837), is a large house offering embroidered tablecloths, thick sweaters, glazed earthenware, and many other products of the country's **handicrafts and popular arts** (branches are at 14 Rennweg and the Kloten Airport).

A little less pretentious than the stores along Bahnhofstrasse are those on Löwenstrasse, west of it, and on the Limmatquai on the river's east bank. Much of what is offered by the smart shops and boutiques of the center may also be found, at more moderate prices, along Langstrasse in the lower-middle-class Aussersihl section, which on some blocks has a Mediterranean flavor. (Take the No. 8 tram from Paradeplatz to Helvetiaplatz stop.)

An **outdoor market** with all kinds of merchandise is held in the Helvetiaplatz from early morning to 9 P.M. on the last Thursday in the months of April, June, August, and October. The **Marktplatz** in the northeastern Oerlikon section near the railroad station (several S-Bahn lines run from Hauptbahnhof) is a suburban shopping center popular with neighborhood residents as well as with visitors staying in the business and convention hotels between Oerlikon and Kloten Airport.

A weekly outdoor market is held on the Limmatquai every Saturday from early morning to 4 P.M. Browsers may be interested in the odds and ends displayed at the weekly **flea market** in Bürkliplatz at the lake end of Bahn-hofstrasse, every Saturday from morning to about 4 P.M., but don't expect to discover any valuable item that Zurich's savvy art merchants might have overlooked.

Among the **bookshops** are Librairie Payot, 9 Bahn-hofstrasse (2115452), which has a selection of English-language and, above all, French books; it is closed on Monday mornings. Specializing in old books are ABC Antiquariat, 31 Zähringerstrasse (2527145), in the Nieder-dorf section, and other shops in the neighborhood. For scientific and art books, comb the bookshops along Rämi-strasse. Consult the Zurich telephone directory under *Anti-quariate* and *Buchhandlungen*.

As an international center of the **arts and antiques trade,** Zurich boasts some two hundred private galleries. Many are in the Old Town on either bank of the Limmat. Consult the Zurich telephone directory under *Galerien* and *Kunsthandlungen*. The frequent private auctions are adver-tised in the *Neue Zürcher Zeitung*, Switzerland's most pres-tigious daily.

When buying antiquities or non-Swiss works of art, request a certificate of origin. If you have an invoice, you will not run into any trouble when taking your purchase out of Switzerland, but customs officials in other countries may want to know how it got to Zurich in the first place. Police, art officials, and experts in various countries assert that stolen or illegally acquired historical trophies and art objects are often shipped to Switzerland by diplomatic pouch (exempt from customs controls) or smuggled there to be put up for sale in Zurich.

SIDE TRIPS

Küsnacht on the "Gold Coast" of the lake's eastern shore, some four miles (6.5 kilometers) from Zurich's center, is an opulent suburb with a bathing beach, a meticulously kept park near the water, fountains, and many ornate mansions. The fastest way to reach it by public transport is to take the S-7 train from Hauptbahnhof or Stadelhofen railroad station near the Opera House. The Küsnacht village church is from the fifteenth century.

Many writers, artists, and intellectuals lived or live in Küsnacht permanently or during the summer months. Carl Gustav Jung (1875–1961), the psychologist and psychiatrist, resided and died in Küsnacht and is buried in its cemetery (p. 77). The C.G. Jung Institute for Analytical Psychology is at 28 Hornweg, CH-8700 Küsnacht (9105323). Leading restaurants in the village are Petermann's Kunststuben (p. 40) and Le Pavillon of the Ermitage Hotel (p. 39).

Rapperswil, the charming "Town of Roses," dominated by a restored thirteenth-century castle, occupies a short peninsula on the northeastern shore of Lake Zurich, 18 miles (29 kilometers) from the city. The trip from Zurich to Rapperswil takes about forty minutes by S-7 train from Hauptbahnhof or Stadelhofen station and two hours by lake boat from Bürkliplatz.

Called "Rappi" by its many aficionados, the town goes back to prehistoric and Roman settlements and has belonged to the Canton St. Gall since 1803. The Old Town near the castle and the Roman Catholic parish church, which was rebuilt after a fire in 1882, are well preserved: there are a stately town hall, a main square with a fountain, and quaint ancient houses.

The castle complex includes rose gardens and vineyards. A long terrace, overlooking the gardens, commands a fine view of the town, the lake, and the Alps; deer wander in the park. The third floor of the castle houses the **Muzeum Polskie,** Switzerland's Polish Museum (055-275602), with memorabilia of such personages as Chopin and Madame Curie (Maria Sklodowska), and exhibits on Polish culture and Polish émigrés. The museum was founded by the nineteenth-century Polish collector Count Wladyslaw Broel-Plater. Open daily 10 A.M. to noon and 2 to 5 P.M., May to September; 2 to 5 P.M. Sunday, November to March.

Rapperswil's **town museum** (Heimatmuseum, 055-277164), a collection of ancient Roman finds as well as of documents and objects illustrating local history since the Middle Ages, is located in a remnant of the old fortifications. Open 2 to 5 P.M. Saturday to Thursday.

The leading hotel is Schwanen, 12 Seequai (055-219181), on the lakefront; double rooms with bath range from $100 to $130. Speer, 5 Bahnhofplatz (055-273131), is a small house near the railroad station with doubles at $75. The tourist information number at Seequai is 055-277000.

Uetliberg is another popular destination. This hill west of Lake Zurich, 2,867 feet (874 meters) high, is a favorite with Zurichers who like hiking or just want to breathe relatively clean air and enjoy a vast panorama when their city is shrouded in fog or smog. Footpaths climb the Uetliberg from various neighborhoods in the west of Zurich, particularly from the Albisgütli section (No. 13 tram from Hauptbahnhof to last stop). The most comfortable way of ascending the Uetliberg is by S-10 train from the main rail terminal.

The orange-colored trains of the S-10 line, also known as the Uetliberg Railway, depart from Hauptbahnhof every half hour and reach the hill's summit in twenty-five minutes. The curving route, 5.6 miles (9 kilometers) long, includes steep stretches rising 70 feet (21.3 meters) every 1,000 feet (305 meters), making the 120-year-old railroad, which runs on standard-gauge track without any rack or funicular assist, an enduring monument to nineteenth-century engineering.

After seven stops the trains arrive at the Uetliberg terminal at an altitude of 2,667 feet (813 meters). A playground is nearby. The Gratstrasse (Ridge Street) passes a television tower (left), leading to the highest point of the hill, known as Uto-Kulm. An iron belvedere there is 98 feet (30 meters) high, with 167 steps. The panorama from its top embraces the city, the lake, the surrounding hills, and many Alpine peaks. The view is well worth the small admission fee to the belvedere.

Nearby are some restaurants and refreshment stands, including Uto-Kulm (4636676), with guest rooms, and Uto-Staffel (4634222).

Return to Zurich by S-10, or walk down to the Albisgütli section and the No. 13 tram or to some other point on the western outskirts of Zurich. Determined hikers proceed south for about an hour and a half along the Gratstrasse across forests to a point at 2,590 feet (790 meters) altitude, called Felsenegg (Rocky Corner). From there a funicular descends to the suburban village of Adliswil on the Sihl River. (The Adliswil–Felsenegg funicular belongs to Zurich's regional transit network.) From the Adliswil railroad station S-4 trains run to Zurich's main rail terminal.

3.

Basel

BASEL

To Basel-Mulhouse
EuroPort

To Rhine River Port
and Three-Countries Point

Freiburg,
Germany

F R A N C E

Mulhouse, France
Colmar, France

G E R M A N Y

Black Forest

Jura Mountains

N

0 KM .5
0 MILES .25

BADEN
RAILROAD
TERMINAL

FAIRGROUNDS ■

Rhine

MITTLERE BRÜCKE
(MIDDLE BRIDGE)

Augst and
Kaiseraugst
(Augusta
Raurica)

SPALEN GATE ■

⑧ ③

① ② PFALZ
⑦

④

⑤

⑥ ■

■ ⑨

Dornach

BASEL
ZOOLOGICAL
GARDEN ■

BANK FOR
■ INTERNATIONAL
SETTLEMENTS

BAHNHOF
SBB

① Freie Strasse	④ Barfüsserplatz	⑦ Münster
② Münsterplatz	⑤ St. Alban Graben	⑧ City Hall
③ Marketplatz	⑥ Kunstmuseum	⑨ Church of St. Alban

THE SECOND CITY of Switzerland, with a population of around 200,000, is generally considered the country's community with the greatest, though unostentatious, wealth. It is the home of proud patrician and burgher families that for generations have done well in business, built stately houses, collected beautiful objects, and contributed to scholarship and the arts.

Basel (French: Bâle) today houses the corporate headquarters and research laboratories of chemical and pharmaceutical giants. It is a financial center and holds one of Europe's major industrial fairs every autumn. Above all the city prides itself on its museums and commercial art galleries. Basel's river port handles a sizable portion of Switzerland's foreign trade, and the nearby tank farms store much of the oil that the landlocked country imports.

The city owes its very existence and a good deal of its old-money prosperity to the Rhine. This bend, where one of Europe's great rivers sharply turns northward and becomes navigable for large boats, was the site of prehistoric settlements. Celtic traders and shippers forwarded merchandise to and from the Roman Empire at this point, and a general of Julius Caesar founded a stronghold and town 7.5 miles (12 kilometers) upstream (p. 142). The role of this stronghold was taken over centuries later by the settlement on the elbow of the river (Baselers speak of the Rhine "knee"). The first mention of the Latin name Basilia is found in a report by the Roman historian Ammianus Marcellinus on a visit there by Valentinian I, emperor of the West, in A.D. 374.

Medieval Basel was the see of powerful bishops who eventually became territorial rulers. A reminder of the long tenure of episcopal government is Basel's coat of arms: the outline of a bishop's crosier. From 1431 to 1447 the city served as host to a church council. The great assembly of prelates and theologians, the seventeenth ecumenical council according to Roman Catholic reckoning, was a futile attempt at reforming the Church of Rome. It brought much business and money to the city on the Rhine.

Basel became an early center of the new art of book printing, attracting many scholars who wanted to see their writings published. The most famous of them was Erasmus of Rotterdam; the Dutch humanist lived in the city from 1521 to 1529.

In 1501 Basel had joined the Swiss Confederation, and it soon took part in the Protestant Reformation movement. In 1835, in a conflict between the urban residents and the people in the villages of the Canton Basel, the territory split into two autonomous half cantons, Basel-City and Basel-Country.

Basel is the seat of Switzerland's oldest university, which opened in 1460. Among the many renowned scholars who taught at the university was the German philosopher Friedrich Nietzsche; he held the chair of Greek philology in 1869–79 and wrote some of his works in the city. In addition to the academic complex in Basel's core, with a modern administrative center at 1 Petersplatz (2673111), university departments and institutes are scattered throughout the city.

In 1897 the first Zionist Congress took place in Basel. In the concert hall of the Stadt-Casino (which no longer exists; compare p. 118) Theodor Herzl, the champion of modern Zionism, presided over a gathering of Jewish delegates from all over Europe and North America. Herzl was to write in his diary: "In Basel I have founded the Jewish state."

The Bank of International Settlements has had its seat in Basel since its foundation in 1930. Originally created for transactions arising from Germany's reparation payments after World War I, the institution is now a world clearinghouse and a meeting place for the central bankers of the major powers.

WEDGED BETWEEN THE wooded ridges of the Jura Mountains to the southwest and the borders of France and Germany just a streetcar ride from its center, Basel is at an altitude of 895 feet (273 meters), among Switzerland's lowest areas. The climate is relatively mild. Atmospheric and river pollution are local hazards, but some progress has been made in cleaning up both the air that Baselers breathe and the waters of the Rhine. The big river flowing under the bridges looks dark gray with green undertones.

The Alemannic dialect spoken in Basel is different from Zurich's. Natives of the two cities identify one another immediately by the way they speak Swiss-German and often humorously or seriously profess coolness toward the other place and its people. Influences on Basel from nearby Alsace and France in general have been strong over the centuries. Some Baselers have French names, but, thumbing through the city's telephone directory, one notes many Italian listings as well.

ARRIVAL AND DEPARTURE

Basel shares an international airport with the French city of Mulhouse. Opened in 1970, EuroAirport Basel-Mulhouse, on French territory 7.5 miles (12 kilometers) from the center of Basel, is linked with the Swiss city by an international expressway, Flughafenstrasse. Under a special treaty between France and Switzerland, persons traveling between Basel and the airport are exempt from French controls. A call can be placed to the airport from Basel over the local telephone network without using a French area code. The airport information number is 3252511; general airport switchboard, 3253111.

Lately the German city of Freiburg im Breisgau has stepped up connections with Basel-Mulhouse; hence its new label, EuroAirport. It is busy with frequent flights to and from Zurich, Geneva, Paris, London, Frankfurt, and other European hubs. Coaches between the interregional airport and Basel's central railroad terminal, Bahnhof SBB (discussed in the next paragraph), run every twenty or thirty minutes from 5 A.M. to midnight; the fare is $1.30. Also, No. 50 bus runs to the airport from Kannenfeldplatz on Basel's northern outskirts and vice versa. A cab ride from the airport to downtown Basel costs around $14.

Basel is a major European railroad hub, connected with Zurich, Frankfurt, Paris, Geneva, and Milan by frequent trains. Basel's three railroad terminals for passengers are Bahnhof SBB (Swiss Federal Railways Terminal), 20 Centralbahnstrasse (information, 2726767), three-fifths of a

mile (about a kilometer) from the left bank of the Rhine
and a fifteen-minute walk from the city center; Bahnhof
SNCF (French National Railways Terminal) in the same
complex (information, 2715032); and Badischer Bahnhof
DB (Baden Terminal of the German Federal Railways),
200 Schwarzwaldallee (information, 6913373), on the
northeastern outskirts of the city, not quite a mile (1.5
kilometers) from the right bank of the Rhine.

The three passenger terminals, the vast freight terminals, the shipping areas, and the river port are all linked by
rail. No fewer than 7 percent of the 14 square miles (36
square kilometers) of the Half Canton of Basel-City are
taken up by trackage.

Between Basel Bahnhof SBB and Zurich Hauptbahnhof there are two trains in both directions every hour from
early morning to late at night. Trains between Basel and
Geneva run hourly.

The Swiss national motorways N-3 from Zurich and
Baden and N-2 from Lucerne, Bern, and Geneva join a
few miles east of Basel. The merged motorway has exits
in the south and east of the city, bypasses the center, skirts
the Baden Terminal in a tunnel, and proceeds into Germany and France.

For assistance in a mechanical breakdown, call 140
(Strassenhilfe) or 3120117 (Pannenhilfe, Automobil-Club
der Schweiz); for other automotive matters, contact Touring-
Club der Schweiz, 13 Steinentorstrasse (27211955), at the
city center. To summon a second driver in case of excessive
alcohol consumption, call Lotsendienst, Taxi-Zentrale,
2712222.

Near the right-bank exits from the N-2 Motorway
are a number of large parking garages: Muba-Parking,
Riehenstrasse near the fairgrounds, with space for 1,400
cars; Bahnhof Parking, near the Baden Terminal, for 620

cars; Jelmoli Parking, Rebgasse, in the Jelmoli department store complex, 300 cars. Parking garages close to the left bank and the center are Storchen-Parking, Fischmarkt, for 200 cars; and Elisabethen-Parking, off Steinenberg-Strasse, 860 cars.

TRANSPORTATION

A network of green **trams, trolley cars, and buses** covers the city and extends into outlying districts. The fare is about 70¢ for rides up to four stops, $1.30 for longer rides with free transfers. A day ticket at around $4.30 is good for any number of rides during a twenty-four-hour period. Buy tickets from the vending machines at the stops. Day tickets can also be bought from the sales offices of the Basel Transit System (Basler Verkehrsbetriebe, BVB)—for instance, in the subterranean shopping mall near Bahnhof SBB—and at many hotels. Before the first ride validate the day ticket at a vending machine. For information on Basel mass transit, call BVB, 2678991.

In addition to the six bridges spanning the Rhine in Basel, four **public ferries** connect the riverbanks between the bridges; a ferryboat ride costs 68¢ for adults, 48¢ for children.

Taxi ranks are near the railroad terminals and big hotels. For radio-dispatched cabs, call Taxi-Zentrale, 2712222, for small cabs, Mini-Taxi, 2711111. Taxi and limousine service can also be requested from one of the firms listed in the Basel telephone directory under *Taxis*.

A **sightseeing coach** with a multilingual guide leaves from the Victoria Hotel, 3–4 Centralbahnplatz (2715566), near Bahnhof SBB, at 10 A.M. daily for a city tour lasting one hour and forty-five minutes. The fare is $12.15 for adults, half price for children. Many landmarks can also be easily reached on foot.

Large **riverboats** of the Rhine Navigation Company take passengers to the Basel river port (p. 130), the Roman ruins at Kaiseraugst (p. 142), and such foreign destinations as Mulhouse in France and Breisach in Germany. Drinks, snacks, and full meals are available on board. The boats sail from the left-bank Schifflände, near the Middle Bridge (p. 119). For information, contact Basler Personenschiffahrt, 2 Blumenrain (2612400).

River buffs may travel from Basel down the Rhine all the way to the Dutch seaport of Rotterdam in big, modern boats. The long-distance passenger boats sail several times a week from the left-bank Rhine port in the St. Joseph section near the Swiss-French border. The voyage, with stops in major Rhine ports, takes three to four days. Information is available from KD German Rhine Line (the *KD* stands for Köln-Düsseldorf), Elsässer Rheinweg (3225809), or from travel agencies.

ACCOMMODATIONS

One top-rated establishment in the city center, overlooking the Rhine, claims to be Switzerland's oldest hotel (see entry for Drei Könige am Rhein). There are a dozen other five-star and four-star houses as well as less expensive places in Basel and its immediate surroundings, with a total of 4,300 guest beds. During the Swiss Trade Fair in spring, the important Autumn Fair, and periodic special events in the fairgrounds, it isn't easy to find accommodation in or near the city. Some exhibitors and fairgoers commute from Zurich, Strasbourg, or Stuttgart.

The Basel Tourist Board, 2 Blumenrain (2615050,

fax 2615944), or Basel Hotelreservation, 7 Messeplatz (6917700, fax 6912005), will assist in the search for a room. Or inquire at City Information at Bahnhof SBB (2713684) during office hours. Travelers arriving on the A-5/N-2 Motorway will find a City Information office at the Basel/ Weil roadhouse near the Swiss-German border.

Following is a list of selected hotels. Quality and service are also generally satisfactory in houses not cited here.

Five-star Houses ($195 to $390 for a double room, continental breakfast included)

Drei Könige am Rhein (Three Kings on the Rhine), 8 Blumenrain (2615252, fax 2612153). When the elegant neoclassical building near the Middle Bridge went up in 1842, it replaced an inn that dated back to the Middle Ages; hence the hotel's boast to be the oldest in the country. The "three kings" said to have lodged at the spot (at different times) were Emperor Conrad II (990–1039), his son Henry II (973–1024), and the last king of Burgundy, Rudolph III (993–1032). What is certain is that several other potentates and Napoleon (in 1797) slept in the old "Three Kings." In today's hotel the rooms and suites on the river side are much in demand. The good, French-style restaurant also looks out on the Rhine.

Euler Manz Privacy, 14 Centralbahnplatz (2724500, fax 2715000), near Bahnhof SBB, is a favorite haunt of the international bankers who periodically meet in Basel. Renowned restaurant (p. 110).

Basel Hilton, 31 Aeschengraben (2716622, fax 2715220), near the Bank of International Settlements and Bahnhof SBB, is the city's second-biggest hotel with 354 beds in

more than 200 rooms and suites, two restaurants, a discotheque, a sauna, and an outdoor swimming pool. The
Hilton is favored by business executives.

Swissôtel Le Plaza, 25 Am Messeplatz (6923333, fax
6915633), Basel's biggest and newest hotel, is near the
fairgrounds. Geared to business clients, it has conference
rooms, a covered swimming pool, and a nightclub.

Four-star Houses ($90 to $230 for a double room)

Victoria am Bahnhof, 3–4 Centralbahnplatz (2715566,
fax 2715501), faces the SBB Terminal. Comfortable, with
efficient service and a good restaurant.

Der Teufelhof, 47 Leonhardsgraben (2611010, fax
2611004), is in the trendy Spalen section. This unconven-
tional establishment describes itself as an "art hotel" and
has only eight double-bed rooms. Its other amenities include two restaurants (p. 110), a modern café and bar
looking out on a garden, two small theaters (p. 132), and
an "archeological cellar" with excavations. Each guest
room in the thoroughly revamped old building is periodically redecorated by a modern artist. The sinister name
Teufelhof (Devil's Court) was taken from an old theatrical
café in a nearby square that the owners once managed.

Merian am Rhein, 2 Rheingasse (6810000, fax 6811101),
on the right bank of the river, is near the Middle Bridge.
This modern house has a terrace overlooking the Rhine,
two restaurants, and a café.

Schweizerhof, 1 Centralbahnplatz (2712833, fax 2712919),
opposite the SBB Bahnhof, is a reliable commercial place.

Three-star Houses ($70 to $176 for a double room)

Gotthard-Terminus, 13 Centralbahnstrasse (2715250, fax 2715214), is opposite the SBB rail terminal. No restaurant. A busy commercial establishment.

Krafft am Rhein, 12 Rheingasse (6918877, no fax), on the right bank near the Middle Bridge, is a quiet hotel.

Spalenbrunnen, 2 Schützenmattstrasse (2618233, fax 2610037), is a small house (forty-five beds) in the Spalen section in the city's north.

Two-star Selection

Bristol, 15 Centralbahnstrasse (2713822, fax 2713845), opposite the SBB rail terminal, is a rather plain hotel with a restaurant. Double rooms cost between $110 and $125; without private bath, they range from $75 to $95. Breakfast included.

One-star Selection

Hecht am Rhein, 8 Rheingasse (6912220, fax 6810788), is close to Krafft am Rhein and has a restaurant and nightclub. Doubles are $90 to $120; without private bath, $65 to $75. Breakfast included.

Rooms and Apartments

For short- and medium-term rentals, consult the Basel telephone directory under *Pensionen* (boardinghouses), *Aparthotel* and *Apartementhäuser* (apartment houses with or without hotel services).

Youth Hostel

Youth Hostel, 10 St. Alban-Kirchrain (2720572), is in a former silk-ribbon factory in the fashionable St. Alban section. Membership card of the International Youth Hostel Federation is required; 150 beds. Closed December 16 to January 31.

Camping Site

Camping Waldhort, 16 Heideweg, Reinach (7116429), is in a wildlife refuge about 5 miles (8 kilometers) south of Basel near Route No. 18, Basel–Delémont. Dornach with the Goetheanum is nearby. Open March to October.

EATING OUT

Basel food is a blend of Alsatian and Alemannic-Swiss cooking, influenced, especially in high-class eating places, by classic French cuisine. Sausages, ham, Zurich-style veal and potatoes, Swabian dumplings (Spätzle, which are small dumplings), and Alsatian *choucroûte garnie* (ham, lard, sausages, and sauerkraut) are common offerings.

Alsatian wines are popular, but Baselers are particularly proud of their local beer. Feldschlösschen, with a large brewery at the spa of Rheinfelden near Basel that looks like a red-brick castle, is well liked. Some Baselers, however, swear that the product of their own Warteck Brewery (79 Grenzacherstrasse, 6957711) on the right bank of the Rhine is Switzerland's best. A right-bank Basel restaurant, Fischerstube (p. 112), draws mild beer from its own mini-brewery.

Whenever Baselers are questioned about their local culi-

nary specialties, they will be at a loss or perhaps say "Leck-
erli" (also spelled Läckerli). These are cookies baked with
honey and almonds, now mostly made commercially for
the tourist trade. The more expensive confections come in
pretty boxes designed by local artists and destined to become lasting souvenirs.

Top Restaurants

Stucki Bruderholz, 42 Bruderholzallee (358222, fax
358203), is in a well-to-do neighborhood on a hill on the
city's south side (No. 15 tram from the center). This is
Basel's leading place for haute cuisine, one of Switzerland's
four or five top restaurants. Owner-chef Hans Stucki and
his wife, Susi, have over the years experimented with nouvelle cuisine and have won plaudits from authoritative culinary critics. Stucki creatively continues using the day's
fresh market and import supplies. Oysters, foie gras, freshwater and sea fish, and delicate meat dishes are always on
the menu. The desserts are superb, and the wine list is
impressive. Patrons are seated in three lavishly decorated
rooms and in summer may start with drinks in a flower
garden with a view of the hillside. Fixed-price lunches or
dinners for two with a good bottle of wine range from
$200 to $300. Closed Sunday and Monday. Reserve early.

Euler, 14 Centralbahnplatz (2724500), in the Euler hotel
(p. 106), is renowned for its classic French cuisine; the
house specialty is seafood. Dinner for two with wine from
the capacious cellar will cost up to $200.

Teufelhof, 47 Leonhardsgraben and 30 Heuberg (2611010),
is in the Teufelhof hotel (p. 107). A soberly elegant
restaurant and a bright wine tavern serve French-oriented
gastronomic creations. The wine list is an awe-inspiring

thirty-eight-page brochure. Meals for two run from $75 to $280. The restaurant is closed Monday and Tuesday, whereas the wine tavern is open daily.

Other Outstanding Eating Places

Additional hotel restaurants: **Drei Könige am Rhein** (p. 106) has a river terrace and French-inspired cuisine; lunch or dinner for two, $60 to $150. **Victoria** (p. 107) offers full meals or snacks, up to $60 for two. **Café Spitz,** in the Merian hotel (p. 107), has a river view. Full meals for two at around $50.

Kunsthalle, 7 Steinenberg (2724233), in an exhibition complex (p. 126), has a terrace, a garden, a full-fledged restaurant, and an informal section. This is a place for snacks, light meals, or more substantial fare. Full meals for two cost around $40. Open daily until midnight.

Chez Donati, 48 St. Johanns-Vorstadt (3220919), is in the city's north near the left bank of the Rhine (No. 15 tram). Franco Donati's charming place with a terrace overlooking the river is widely renowned for its blend of Italian and French cooking. Dinner for two is about $60. Closed Monday and all July.

Schlüsselzunft, 25 Freie Strasse (2612046), is in the fifteenth-century building of the locksmiths' guild on Basel's main shopping street. Swiss cuisine; dinner for two, $50 to $60. Closed Sunday.

Storchen, 10 Fischmarkt (2612929), is centrally located, with a terrace and garden. Lunch or dinner for two, $40 to $60. Closed Sunday.

Grand Café Huguenin, 6 Barfüsserplatz (2720550), is centrally located, with a sidewalk terrace. No alcoholic

drinks; warm food until 5 P.M., open until 7 P.M. daily.
Popular for light lunches, snacks, cappuccino, and ice
cream.

Zum Braunen Mutz, 10 Barfüsserplatz (2613369). The
name of this brasserie means "at the sign of the brown
bear"; it occupies an ancient building with a frescoed facade
on a central square, Barfüsserplatz (p. 117). Alsatian sausages, freshwater fish, snacks. Lunch for two with beer,
around $30.

Fischerstube, 45 Rheingasse (6926635), is on a street lined
with old houses off the Middle Bridge on the right bank.
Four different beers of the Ueli trademark from the local
brewery on the premises are drawn fresh from their casks.
It seems that a Dr. Hans Nidecker founded the enterprise
as a hobby. Sausages, rumpsteaks, and trout are some of
the food offerings. Lunch or dinner for two, around $50.

St. Alban-Eck, 60 St. Albanvorstadt (2710320), is near the
Museum of Fine Arts and is convenient for visitors to that
institution. A historic place with Swiss and French cuisine.
Lunch or dinner for two, up to $80. Closed Sunday.

Solitude Parkrestaurant, 206 Grenzacherstrasse (6815252),
is a bucolic place on the right bank of the Rhine on the
eastern outskirts, with its own parking lot. (No. 31 bus.)
French cuisine with an accent on fish. Lunch or dinner for
two, around $80. Closed Saturday and after 6 P.M. Sunday
and Monday.

Asian Food

Chinese cuisine: **Hongkong,** 91 Riehenring (6918814), is
near the fairgrounds. Cantonese dishes. Lunch or dinner

for two will cost up to $60. Closed Monday. Reservations recommended during the spring and autumn fairs and special exhibitions.

Japanese restaurant: **Sakura,** 14 Centralbahnstrasse (2720505), is in the rail terminal complex. Full meals for two, up to $100.

Kosher Food

Topas, 24 Leimenstrasse (2718700), is in the Jewish Community house adjoining the Synagogue. Warm dishes are served until 9 P.M. Reservations required for Friday night and on Jewish holidays.

Self-Service and Fast Food

MIGROS Restaurants (compare p. 48) are at 8 Untere Rebgasse (6812777), on the right bank of the Rhine, near the Middle Bridge; and at 19 Henric Petri-Strasse (2721915), near the Stadttheater.

McDonald's has branches at 13 Centralbahnstrasse (2728300), near SBB rail terminal; 9 Barfüsserplatz (2719033), central; 15 Greifengasse (6812262), on the right bank near the Middle Bridge.

Snack bars and refreshment stands will be found in the department stores and in the railroad terminals.

Cafés

Confiserie Schiesser, 19 Marktplatz (2616077), is a Basel institution. The tearoom on the second floor, with old-fashioned wainscoted decor and a view of the frescoed facade of City Hall opposite, is a place for gossiping over tea or coffee with croissants or pastry from the confectionery below.

Café Pfalz, 11 Münsterberg (2726511), near the Cathedral.

Café Gfeller, 9 Eisengasse (2613540), central location, also for snacks and light lunches.

Café Merkur, 5 Post-Passage (2721120), in the impressively modern Post Office building adjoining the SBB rail terminal, also has a terrace.

Picnic Food

Shop in the food courts of the department stores. Fresh fruits can be bought at the outdoor stands in Marktplatz.

WHAT TO SEE

A stroll around the Old Town and a few hours in the Museum of Fine Arts (Kunstmuseum) are musts; one day will be sufficient for getting a superficial impression. To do justice to Basel, which likes to describe itself as "the cultural heart of Switzerland," the visitor should also see the other public collections and some of the private art galleries; the popular "Zolli," Switzerland's largest zoo; the busy river port near the Swiss-French-German border; and the Roman ruins and museum of Augst. A determined sightseer will be kept busy for at least three days.

The Old Town

For a good start, climb the low hill on which the **Cathedral** (Münster) rises. From the terrace behind it look out on the

Rhine. This belvedere is known as the *Pfalz*; the German word is derived from the Latin term for *palace*. An ancient Roman military base existed on the spot, which in the early Middle Ages became the bishop's residence. The strategic hill dominates the river bend and today commands an impressive panorama of Lesser Basel across the river and, downstream, of the Rhine port, the buildings and smokestacks of the industrial district, and the heights of the Black Forest and the Jura on the horizon.

The Münster—this word originally meant *monastery church*—was the see, or cathedral, of the bishops of Basel until the Protestant Reformation came to the city in 1521–29. Today the Münster serves as the parish church of Basel's principal Evangelical-Reformed community.

The red sandstone edifice, which turns its rear (the choir) toward the Rhine, dates from the twelfth century. It replaced an earlier church that was probably destroyed by Magyar warriors from the Danube lowlands when they penetrated to the Rhine and raided the town on its bend in A.D. 916. The oldest parts of the present structure are in Romanesque style with Gothic additions. After an earthquake gravely damaged the church in 1356, it was rebuilt in the Gothic style over the next 150 years.

The upper portions of the two front towers and the apse are Gothic. Four sculptures on the west facade represent Emperor Saint Henry II (973–1024), founder of the original church; his Empress, Saint Kunigunde (right); the Tempter; and one of the Foolish Virgins of Christ's parables (left).

The so-called St. Gall Portal on the north side (left of the main facade) is in the original late-Romanesque style, its sculptures representing the Evangelists, Jesus with saints Peter and Paul, the Wise and the Foolish Virgins, and other religious themes. A rose window is in the shape of a wheel of fortune. The Cathedral is adjoined, on its south side, by a large double-cloister with old tombs and commemorative inscriptions.

The interior, with five aisles, contains a fourteenth-century bishop's throne, a fifteenth-century baptismal font, and a pulpit. In the apse are the tombs of the thirteenth-century Queen Gertrude Anna of Habsburg, wife of King Rudolf I, the founder of the dynasty of Habsburg kings and emperors who would rule for more than six centuries, and of their son, Karl. The red marble tombstone of Erasmus of Rotterdam, who lived in Basel from 1521 to 1529, is in the northern side aisle. Stained-glass paintings are from the nineteenth century.

The elongated square in front of the Cathedral, **Münsterplatz,** is lined with stately old houses. The harmonious space has for centuries been the scene of popular and civic celebrations. An antiques market is held in the square every Saturday.

From the Münster descend to **Freie Strasse** (Free Street), Basel's principal shopping area (closed to motor traffic), and proceed northward to **Marktplatz** (Market Square). "Märt" to the natives, it is the core of present-day Basel. A colorful outdoor market with vegetables, fruits, cheeses, and flower stands is held in the square every weekday morning; some of the produce is supplied by nearby Alsace (France).

On the square's northeastern side rises Basel's **City Hall,** recently repaired and now again resplendent in red and gold, as well as the **Civic Tower.** The central portion of City Hall, with Gothic arcades, is nearly five hundred years old. The battlements bordering the steep roof carry the coats of arms of Swiss cantons; the figures above the big clock represent Emperor Henry II and Empress Kunigunde. The Civic Tower on the right of City Hall complex and a high wing on the left side, both in the style of the original structure, were added between 1898 and 1900.

The frescoed courtyard encloses a seventeenth-century statue of the ancient Roman dignitary Lucius Munatius Plancus, whom Baselers like to consider the founder of their city. Plancus, mentioned by Cicero and other Roman writers, was a general of Julius Caesar and an enemy of Queen Cleopatra; as governor of northern Gaul in 44–43 B.C., he established a veterans' colony at what is now Augst (p. 142) upstream of Basel.

The Hall of the Grand Council was frescoed by Hans Holbein the Younger in 1521–22 and, after he had been appointed as the official town painter, in 1530. Guided visits of the Grand Council Hall and other rooms of City Hall are conducted by the Basel Tourist Board at 3 P.M. every Tuesday; the fee is $5.50.

Turn around in the Marktplatz and by way of Gerbergasse and Falknerstrasse, both roughly parallel to Freie Strasse, proceed to **Barfüsserplatz.** Several tramlines converge on this traffic hub, the former hog market, which derives its present name from the church on its southeast side.

Barfüsser Kirche (also written as Barfüsserkirche; Church of the Barefoot Ones) takes its name from the austere discalced Franciscans. The Gothic church, built in the early fourteenth century, adjoined a Franciscan monastery that no longer exists. The Barfüsser Kirche is now the seat of Basel's **Historical Museum** (p. 124).

A small tributary of the Rhine, the **Birsig River,** flows underground in most of the central city including Barfüsserplatz and Falknerstrasse.

From the square an underpass, Theater-Passage, leads to the new **Stadttheater** (Civic Theater), a large, modern structure opened in 1974. Its concrete walls are often cov-

ered with graffiti (in tidy Switzerland!). In front of the
theater is a pond with mobiles by the Swiss sculptor Jean
Tinguely, the Tinguely Brunnen (Tinguely Fountain), also
called Carnival Fountain. Its weird machines have been
busily rotating, seesawing, and spewing water since 1977.

Opposite Theaterplatz (Theater Square), at 14 Steinenberg, is the new **Stadt-Casino** (p. 131) with halls for
concerts and conventions. The building, opened in 1938,
replaced an early-nineteenth-century Stadt-Casino in
which the first Zionist Congress was held, August 29–31,
1897. A bronze plaque in German and Hebrew recalls the
event.

Walk down Steinenberg to St. Alban Graben, a boulevard along what was once a moat of the city fortifications.
At 16 St. Alban Graben is the **Museum of Fine Arts**
(Kunstmuseum, p. 121), a bright, arcaded building from
the early 1930s that looks like a stripped-down version of
the Ducal Palace in Venice. Before or after visiting this
remarkable institution take a stroll around the newly affluent neighborhood, the **St. Alban's section,** which is dot-
ted with other art collections and private art galleries. A
long, straight street with houses from the eighteenth and
nineteenth centuries, as well as a few older ones, St. Alban-
Vorstadt (St. Alban Suburb) leads to the Gate of St. Alban
(St. Alban-Tor) with a tall, square tower, a remnant of the
ancient bulwarks around the city.

Turn toward the Rhine via a narrow lane, St. Alban-
Kirchrain, to see the little sixteenth-century **Church of St.
Alban** at No. 11, and behind it what has remained of the
nearly one-thousand-year-old monastery of St. Alban to
which the neighborhood owes its name. The Benedictine
monks of the once powerful Cluny branch of their order
who lived here in the Middle Ages developed the area and
dug two canals. These ditches are still visible. For centuries

the waters diverted from the Rhine powered several flour mills and sawmills, and eventually also paper mills and other manufacturing plants.

Behind the Church of St. Alban is a row of columns and Romanesque arches that belonged to the medieval monastery's cloister. The recently redeveloped neighborhood with its Gothic and timber-framed houses has retained an archaic character; the street name Mühlegraben (Mill Ditch) is indicative. One restored historic paper mill, at 35–37 St. Alban-Tal, houses the **Museum of Paper, Writing and Printing** (p. 123).

Another old, and newly fashionable, neighborhood worth visiting is the hilly **Spalen-Vorstadt** northwest of the city core. Take the No. 3 tram from Barfüsserplatz to the Spalentor stop, or walk there by way of Kohlenberg and Leonhardsgraben.

The **Spalen Gate** (Spalentor) used to control access to Basel from Alsace. The massive doorway from the fourteenth century is crowned by a steep roof with green-and-gold tiles and flanked by two crenellated towers.

Walk down Spalen-Vorstadt, a street with Renaissance houses, old-book and antiques shops, private art galleries, and boutiques. At the intersection of Spalen-Vorstadt and Schützenmatt Strasse, note an artistic fountain from the sixteenth century. A frieze above the flower-decorated basin, showing rustics at a dance, is said to be by Hans Holbein the Younger. A figure of a bagpiper tops the fountain.

Lesser Basel

To explore Kleinbasel (Lesser Basel) on the right bank of the Rhine, start from the **Mittlere Brücke** (Middle Bridge). Built at the beginning of the twentieth century, this stone bridge with five arches replaced an often-repaired wooden structure that had spanned the river at the same spot since the thirteenth century. The nucleus of Lesser Basel—Greifengasse from the Middle Bridge to Claraplatz and the blocks on either side—is a shopping neighborhood with department stores, many other businesses, and quaint secondhand places. Turn from the Middle Bridge to the right on the river embankment, **Oberer Rheinweg.** The view from this tree-lined promenade facing the Cathedral on its hill on the opposite bank is magnificent. Most of the buildings on Oberer Rheinweg are from the nineteenth century, but there are also a few much older, narrow houses. Before Wettstein Bridge, upstream of Middle Bridge, turn around and walk back by way of Lindenberg, a low hill with half-timbered buildings from the seventeenth and eighteenth centuries. From Lindenberg the Rheingasse, parallel to the river promenade, runs to Greifengasse; here too are several Gothic and baroque houses.

Beyond the Gothic **Church of St. Clare,** which is Roman Catholic, the straight Clarastrasse leads to the **fairgrounds** (Mustermesse; No. 4 and No. 6 trams from the city center). Commercial fairs have been held here since the fifteenth century, attracting visitors and business to Basel from all over the region and beyond it.

The Swiss Autumn Fair is Switzerland's largest periodic industrial show, and one of Europe's most important. Basel also holds a Swiss Sample Fair (Schweizer Mustermesse) every year in March and a number of specialized international trade exhibitions. The latter include an International Art Fair in late spring, a European Watch and Jewelry Fair, an Office Equipment Fair, an International Electronics Fair, and an International Chemistry Fair. The

Basel fairgrounds also serve as host to a number of international symposiums and conventions. The fairs and conventions bring thousands of exhibitors and more than a million registered visitors each year.

The fairgrounds cover 47 acres (19 hectares), about the size of the United Nations headquarters enclave in New York. Nine-tenths of the fair area are occupied by air-conditioned exhibition halls with escalators and elevators. The main building with administrative offices is at 3 Messeplatz (6862020, fax 5920617); a Congress Center (6862828, fax 691049) is nearby. Sidings allow freight cars to roll into the fairgrounds from the railroad network and the Rhine port.

Museums and Collections

Basel museums are accessible to wheelchair users unless otherwise stated.

Museum of Fine Arts (Kunstmuseum), 16 St. Alban Graben (2710828), is at the approaches to the St. Alban's section. The institution can be reached from the SBB rail terminal by No. 2 tram. Open 10 A.M. to 5 P.M. Tuesday to Sunday. Admission: $2.30, Sunday free. One of Europe's grand art repositories, this is Switzerland's most comprehensive collection of its kind. Its treasures range from Gothic to mid-twentieth-century art. Outstanding are the museum's paintings by Hans Holbein the Younger and its Picassos. The Kunstmuseum also boasts the world's largest collection of paintings by Arnold Böcklin, who was a native of Basel, including *The Plague* and *The Isle of the Dead*.

On entering the courtyard the visitor sees a cast of

Rodin's *The Burghers of Calais* (the original is in Paris) and other modern sculptures including works by Jean Arp and Alexander Calder.

Much of the museum's older section was first assembled by Basilius Auerbach, a Basel jurist and avid collector whose father, Bonifacius, had been close to Erasmus of Rotterdam and the younger Hans Holbein. The city of Basel bought the Auerbach treasure trove in 1661. A vivid likeness of the bearded Bonifacius Auerbach, who also practiced law, by his friend Hans Holbein the Younger hangs near the artist's celebrated portraits of Sir Thomas More (painted in London) and Erasmus on the second floor. There are also works by Hans Holbein the Elder and by his other son, Ambrosius, who died young. Noteworthy in this section are several paintings by the late-Gothic master Konrad Witz, who worked in Basel until his death around 1445; an agonizing Christ on the Cross by Matthias Grünewald; and works by Martin Schongauer and Lucas Cranach the Elder. Among a large group of Flemish and Dutch pictures are some early Rembrandts and landscapes by Jacob van Ruisdael. Italian masters are scarce, and a group of works by European artists of the seventeenth and eighteenth centuries is unexceptional.

The museum's main floor is devoted to the impressionists: many Cézannes, and works by Corot, Courbet, Degas, Gaugin, van Gogh, Manet, Monet, Pissarro, and Renoir. On the way upstairs you pass an enormous electromechanical sculpture by Jean Tinguely that is also a clock.

The top floor houses twentieth-century art, especially a roomful of important Picassos representing all the artist's periods from his work *The Two Brothers* (1905) to his expressionist and cubist paintings. One of the works, *Seated Harlequin* (1923), was bought by public subscription. Picasso was so impressed by Basel's civic effort to secure the painting that he donated some drawings for his epochal *Les Demoiselles d'Avignon* to the Kunstmuseum.

Also remarkable are works by Braque, Chagall, and Juan Gris as well as a collection of Fernand Légers. Well represented are Salvador Dalí, Giorgio De Chirico, Max Ernst, Alberto Giacometti, Jasper Johns, Paul Klee, Oskar Kokoschka, Piet Mondrian, Edvard Munch, and Robert Rauschenberg.

The Kunstmuseum building includes an autonomous **Department of Prints and Drawings** (2721855) with a library and a reading room. Open 9 A.M. to noon and 2 to 6 P.M. Tuesday to Friday, 9 A.M. to noon and 2 to 5 P.M. Saturday. Free admission. The collection contains important drawings by Hans Holbein the Elder and the Younger, Martin Schongauer, and some by Albrecht Dürer, as well as drawings and watercolors by Cézanne, Toulouse-Lautrec, Gauguin, Klee, Picasso, Chagall, and other moderns. Some of the items are on permanent display, whereas others are shown in temporary exhibitions. Scholars may request access to pieces in storage.

Museum of Contemporary Art (Museum für Gegenwartskunst), 60 St. Alban-Rheinweg (2728183), is near the Church of St. Alban. Open 10 A.M. to 5 P.M. Wednesday to Monday. Admission: $2.30, Sunday free. A readapted and enlarged nineteenth-century factory, the building contains works created during the second half of the twentieth century. Visitors to the museum's bright halls see the productions of conceptualists, minimalists, and artists of other tendencies during the last few years. Prominent are works by such Americans as Franz Joseph Kline, Barnett Newman, Mark Rothko, Frank Stella, and Andy Warhol.

Museum of Paper, Writing and Printing/Basel Paper Mill, 35–37 St. Alban-Tal (2729652), is near the Museum

of Contemporary Art. Open 2 to 5 P.M. Tuesday to Sunday. Admission: $5.30, children $3, families $15 maxi-
mum. This restored historic mill, with a waterwheel on
the canal outside, dates back to the fifteenth century. Its
machinery and its old equipment for papermaking can be
observed in action. Visitors watch craftsmen as they found
types, set type, print texts, and bind books.

Museum of Ancient Art and Ludwig Collection, 5
St. Alban Graben (2712202), is diagonally opposite the
Kunstmuseum. Open 10 A.M. to 5 P.M. Tuesday to Sunday. Admission: $2.30, Sunday free. Switzerland's only
institution devoted exclusively to the art of classical antiquity and to archaic art objects from Greece and Italy is
renowned above all for its wealth of Greek vases. The
museum occupies two early-nineteenth-century town-
houses with irregular layouts and a new wing built in the
1960s. Most of the exhibits are gifts from private collectors.

Collection of Caricatures and Cartoons, 9 St. Alban-
Vorstadt (2711336), is near the Kunstmuseum. Open 4 to
6:30 P.M. Wednesday and Saturday, 2 to 4 P.M. Sunday;
also, conducted tours by appointment. Admission: $4.40,
children half price. Original works by twentieth-century
artists from all over the world. Special shows are held
periodically.

Historical Museum, Barfüsserplatz (2710505), is located
in the Barfüsser Kirche. Open 10 A.M. to 5 P.M. Wednesday to Monday. Admission: $2.30, Sunday free. The set-
ting for this collection is itself a worthwhile sight—the
fourteenth-century Franciscan church was restored to its
Gothic severity between 1975 and 1981. The museum,
devoted to Basel's history from a Celtic settlement, around

or before the first century B.C. to the present, also contains precious objects from the Cathedral treasury, medieval and Renaissance sacred art, and a collection of magnificent fifteenth-century tapestries.

Kirschgarten House, 27–29 Elisabethenstrasse (2711333), is about halfway between Barfüsserplatz and SBB rail terminal (No. 2 tram from SBB terminal or the Museum of Fine Arts to the Kirschgarten stop). Open 10 A.M. to 5 P.M. Tuesday to Sunday. Admission: $2.30, Sunday free. This furnished mansion from the late eighteenth century, now an outlying appendage to the Historical Museum, conveys an idea of how wealthy Baselers once used to live. There are also collections of china and faience, toys and wrought-iron objects, clocks and scientific instruments.

Collection of Ancient Musical Instruments, 8 Leonhardstrasse (2710505), is a few blocks west of Barfüsserplatz. Open 2 to 5 P.M. Tuesday and Friday, 10 A.M. to noon and 2 to 5 P.M. Sunday. Admission: $2.30, Sunday free. Switzerland's largest collection of old instruments, an appendage of the Historical Museum, adjoins the Music Academy of the City of Basel. Visitors may listen to the taped sound of many of the four hundred instruments on display.

Museum of Design, 2 Spalenvorstadt (2613006), is near the Spalen Gate (No. 3 tram from Barfüsserplatz to the Lyss stop). Open noon to 7 P.M. Tuesday to Friday, noon to 5 P.M. Saturday and Sunday. Admission: $2.30, Sunday free. The institution, the former Arts and Crafts Museum, organizes exhibitions on a variety of themes related to contemporary everyday culture (consult wall posters and the *Museums* listings in the local newspapers). There are also a 100,000-volume specialized library and a collection of 35,000 posters, mainly from Switzerland, which can be viewed by appointment.

Museum of Architecture, 3 Pfluggässlein (2611413), is off Freie Strasse. Open 10 A.M. to noon and 2 to 6:30 P.M. Tuesday to Friday, 10 A.M. to 4 P.M. Saturday, and 10 A.M. to 1 P.M. Sunday. Admission: $2.30. The six-story concrete-and-glass building, erected in 1959, is dedicated to historical and modern architecture and construction techniques; individual architects and their designs are presented in periodic exhibitions.

Kunsthalle, 7 Steinenberg (2724833), is near the Civic Theater. Open 10 A.M. to 5 P.M. Thursday to Tuesday, 10 A.M. to 9 P.M. Wednesday. Admission: $4, free on Wednesday after 5 P.M. This publicly subsidized private institution organizes about ten modern art shows every year. It has been a European bridgehead for American avant-garde artists, and with its restaurant (p. 111) is a meeting place for people active or interested in the visual arts.

Museum of Natural History, 2 Augustinergasse (2665500), is near the Cathedral. Open 10 A.M. to 5 P.M. Tuesday to Sunday, May to October; 10 A.M. to noon and 2 to 5 P.M. Tuesday to Sunday, November to April. Admission: $2, Sunday free. This collection in a large nineteenth-century building is internationally known, especially for its displays on minerals, dinosaurs and other long-extinct animals, ants, and beetles. At most times visitors can also view special exhibitions.

Museum of Ethnology and Swiss Museum of European Folkways, 2 Augustinergasse and 20 Münsterplatz (2665500), is in the same building as the Natural History Museum and has the same hours. Admission: $2, Sunday free. Oceania (with 32,000 exhibits), Indonesia, and the cultures of native Americans are the main strengths of the vast ethnological section. Many of its objects were brought to Basel by local businessmen, missionaries, and researchers. The section on European folkways, the largest Swiss collection of its kind, contains paintings, sculptures, pottery, utensils, and other items documenting how people live, especially in rural areas.

Toy and Village Museum Riehen, 34 Baselstrasse, Riehen (672829), is in the northeastern suburb of Riehen (No. 6 tram from Barfüsserplatz). Open 2 to 5 P.M. Wednesday and Saturday, 10 A.M. to noon and 2 to 5 P.M. Sunday. Free admission.

The museum is a well-restored house in which the seventeenth-century Basel mayor and diplomat Johann Rudolf Wettstein lived. The toy section is an outpost of the Swiss Museum of European Folkways, with exhibits mainly from the nineteenth century—dollhouses, games, teddy bears, and such. The village section focuses on the wineries found in Riehen, by now little more than a memory.

Jewish Museum of Switzerland, 8 Kornhausgasse (2619514), is in the Spalen section (No. 3 tram from Barfüsserplatz to the Lyss stop, not far from the synagogue). Open 2 to 5 P.M. Monday and Wednesday, 10 A.M. to noon and 2 to 5 P.M. Sunday, or by appointment. Free admission. Switzerland's only public collection of Judaica is small but remarkable for a photo of Theodor Herzl with all the 162 participants in the first Zionist Congress in 1897 and other memorabilia of the event, and exhibits about the long history of Jews in Basel.

Swiss Museum of Sports, 28 Missionsstrasse (2611221), is near the Spalen Gate (No. 3 tram to the Pilgerstrasse stop). Open 10 A.M. to 5 P.M. Monday to Saturday, 10 A.M. to noon and 2 to 5 P.M. Sunday. Guided tours at other times by arrangement. Free admission. The museum displays rudimentary skis, primitive and increasingly sophisticated bicycles from 1820 to the present, equipment for eccentric sports, and tens of thousands of other objects, most of which can be shown only in periodic exhibitions. Also a vast library and picture archives.

Cat Museum, 101 Baselstrasse (672694 or 2619323), is in the Riehen suburb. Open 10 A.M. to noon and 2 to 5 P.M. Sunday; other times by appointment. Admission: $2.40, children $1.70. Assembled by cat fanciers in an old English-style mansion with a garden in which a few live tabbies prowl unself-consciously, this collection includes paintings and postage stamps picturing cats, representations of cats as charms or toys, cat sculptures—some ten thousand objects in all. There is also a mummified cat such as were buried under doorsteps as fetishes in the Middle Ages.

Swiss Museum of Pharmaceutical History, 5 Totengässlein (2617940), is near Marktplatz. Open 9 A.M. to noon and 2 to 5 P.M. Monday to Friday. Free admission. This collection in a city that is an international center of the pharmaceutical industry is located on a winding lane with the odd name Totengässlein (Little Street of the Dead). No. 3 is an old house where Erasmus of Rotterdam lived, and where Paracelsus (Theophrastus von Hohenheim), the sixteenth-century physician, chemist, and alchemist, used to go in and out. Ancient laboratory and pharmacy equipment, old medicines, and related material are on display.

Swiss Museum of Navigation, 4 Wiesendamm (663349). Open 10 A.M. to noon and 2 to 5 P.M. Tuesday, Saturday, and Sunday. Admission: $3.50, children $2.00. The display "Our Way to the Sea" contains models of historic and present-day ships, photos and other material concerning Swiss navigation on the Rhine and on the high seas, nautical equipment, and a slide show.

Random Sights and Strolls

The **Bank for International Settlements** has its seat at 2 Centralbahnplatz (2808080), near the SBB rail terminal. The building, erected in the 1970s, is a landmark of the Aeschen Suburb (Aeschenvorstadt), a neighborhood of broad, busy streets, hotels, and solid buildings from the late nineteenth and the twentieth centuries. It is both a residential and a business district.

The twenty-story concrete-and-glass BIS edifice rests on a broad, round base and tapers into a cylindrical tower. The building has a beige metallic sheen that turns into a golden glow when the sun reflects off it. Officials won't say whether there is any real gold in the bank's safes, but the institution usually has plenty of liquidity and is able to arrange quick loans to member banks in emergencies. No casual visitors are admitted; the Bank for International Settlements is proverbially secretive. You must prove you have legitimate business to be allowed into its halls and offices.

The **zoo** (Basel Zoological Garden), main entrance at 40 Binningerstrasse (2810000), is also near the SBB rail terminal. From the terminal, ride the No. 4 tram to the zoo or go to the short distance on foot (a ten-minute walk to the west). From Marktplatz or Barfüsserplatz take the No. 6 tram to the zoo. The facility is open daily 8 A.M. to 6:30 P.M. in summer, 5:30 P.M. in winter. Admission is $5.50 for adults, around $2 for children.

The Baselers' beloved "Zolli" is Switzerland's biggest zoo. Since its opening in 1874 it has been enlarged repeatedly; it now covers 32 acres (13 hectares), about the size of one of the smaller zoos in the United States (like Chicago's Lincoln Park) and Canada. The little Birsig River flows openly across the zoo area.

The "Zolli" houses more than 4,000 animals of at least 550 species. Many of them live in vast enclosures that simulate their natural habitats. The zoo management is proud of its breeding successes: giraffes, rhinoceroses, gorillas, and other exotic animals were born in captivity during recent years. Young exemplars of some species can almost always be seen.

With its old trees and other greenery the zoo serves also as a general recreation area for Baselers. Small fry may ride ponies or a patient elephant in the Children's Zoo section from April to October. A restaurant and self-service cafeteria are in the zoo park.

Another worthwhile excursion is to the **river port and three-country point.** The Rhine port with its busy docks, cranes, and warehouses can be visited by boat or sightseeing bus (p. 105), or with a tram ride followed by a stroll.

If you want to explore the port area on your own, take the No. 14 tram from Barfüsserplatz or Marktplatz all the way to the last stop. Downstream, on the east and west banks of the Rhine, the headquarters of the Ciba-Geigy and Sandoz corporations are visible. (The third of Basel's Big Three of the pharmaceutical industry, F. Hoffmann–La Roche, has its center upstream, near Solitude Park, compare p. 112.) After crossing the small Wiese River, an east-bank tributary of the Rhine, proceed along Hochberger Strasse and Westquai Strasse for fifteen to twenty minutes to a tall metal pylon on a platform above a pier marking the convergence of the borders of Switzerland, France, and Germany. (The exact site where the three boundaries meet is in the middle of the Rhine.)

Off the Hochberger Strasse, at 4 Wiesendamm, is the **Swiss Museum of Navigation** (p. 128).

BEYOND SIGHTSEEING

Music in Basel

Opera, operetta, and ballet are performed at the **Civic Theater** (Stadttheater), 7 Theaterstrasse (2711133), with 1,210 seats. The ticket office is open 10 A.M. to 1 P.M. and 3:30 to 6:45 P.M. on working days. Ticket reservations can be made by phone, 2711130, 10 A.M. to 5 P.M. A ticket window opens forty-five minutes before each performance, selling available tickets.

Basel has two symphony orchestras; they and visiting musical groups and soloists can be heard in several hundred concerts and recitals every year. The complex where most of the classical-music events take place is the **City Casino** (Stadt-Casino), 14 Steinenberg (2726658), which includes the adjoining Concert Hall, built in 1876. The 1,500-seat Grand Hall, in neobaroque style in white, beige, brown, and gold, has good acoustics. The City Casino also contains two smaller concert halls with 750 and 550 seats. Tickets can be bought at Music School Hug, 70 Freie Strasse (2712323); Au Concert, 24 Aeschenvorstadt (2721176); and other music and record firms. The Stadt-Casino ticket office (2726657) opens an hour before scheduled events.

Classical music is also performed at the **Music Acad-**

emy of the City of Basel, 6 Leonhardstrasse (2615722), with two concert halls (342 and 100 seats). Buy tickets at Au Concert and other music shops.

Organ concerts and other music are offered in the **Church of St. Leonhard,** Leonhards-Kirchplatz near the Music Academy, and in other Basel churches. Watch for announcements in the local press.

Touring pop and rock stars and groups make appearances usually at the **City Casino,** at the **Congress Center** near the fairgrounds, or in the **Sporthalle St. Jakob,** 21 Brüglinger Strasse (3128896; tickets, 3117555), a sports hall adjacent to a stadium on the southeastern outskirts.

Theater

Legitimate drama is often on the program schedule of the **Civic Theater.** The 330-seat **Kleine Bühne** (Little Stage) in the same building frequently produces avant-garde plays.

There are a number of other stages in Basel. **Komödie,** 63 Steinenvorstadt (2711130), is near the Civic Theater and under the same management (650 seats). **Teufelhof,** 47 Leonhardsgraben (2611261; p. 107), has two theaters, one with one hundred seats and a smaller one with flexible seating arrangements. **Théâtre Fauteuil,** 12 Spalenberg (2612610), in the Spalen section, includes a 240-seat theater on the ground floor and **Neues Tabourettli,** with eighty seats, above it. **Piccolo,** 30–32 Ramsteiner Strasse (3126420), east of the St. Alban section, has eighty-five seats, and **Piccolissimo,** in the same building, has fifty seats.

For puppet shows, visit **Basler Marionetten-Theater,** 8 Münsterplatz (2610612), near the Cathedral; 170 seats (dialogue often in Basel dialect).

Scenes from Goethe's *Faust*, as well as other plays, are frequently performed at the **Goetheanum** near Dornach (see p. 145).

Cinema

The winding Steinenvorstadt, two blocks west of the Civic Theater, is Basel's movie street, with several theaters. For programs and other movie houses, consult the telephone directory under *Kinos* and the daily press.

Night Life

Basel's discotheques and other night spots are particularly busy during the Autumn Fair and other international exhibitions and conventions. The mandatory closing time is generally 2 A.M., 3 A.M. Saturday and Sunday nights and during trade fairs. Piano bars and discos are featured at the major hotels, for instance, Drei Könige am Rhein, Euler, and Basel Hilton (p. 106).

Other establishments include Club 59, 33 Steinenvorstadt (2816669), near the Civic Theater, a restaurant with a bar and discotheque; Only One, 2 Clarastrasse (6810007), in Lesser Basel, a big discotheque; and Frisco Bar, 3 Untere Rebgasse (6810990), in Lesser Basel, a striptease place.

Several nightclubs in Weil am Rhein and other German towns near the border that can be easily reached from Basel by taxi, train, bus, or private car cater to Basel fairgoers; their publicity fliers will be found in Basel hotel lobbies.

Folklore

Basel is one of the few Protestant participants in the international parade of exuberant carnival celebrations from

Cologne to Venice to Rio de Janeiro. The Swiss city, unlike most of the Roman Catholic revelers elsewhere, goes on its annual spree *after* Ash Wednesday instead of during the days and nights before it.

Merrymaking in Basel the week after Ash Wednesday has been recorded since the middle of the sixteenth century; it may in the beginning have coincided with, and been occasioned by, the yearly reviews of the citizens' militia. The word for carnival in Basel is, at any rate, *Fasnacht*, a corruption of the German term *Fastnacht*, meaning Shrove Tuesday, the night before the period of ritual fasting, Lent.

At Fasnacht time the Baselers, supposedly so staid, let go and drop the reserve they maintain the rest of the year. During the three carnival days many offices and stores in the city stay closed or have shortened hours while the schedule of municipal streetcars and buses is expanded to include extra early and late runs for the convenience of the carousers. Some young Baselers take advantage of the semiholidays to leave town for the ski slopes.

On the other hand, sightseers flock to the city on the Rhine from all over Switzerland and from nearby Alsace and Germany to gawk at the frolicking and maybe take part in it. Basel, at all other times a most hospitable place, doesn't actually discourage tourists from coming for Fasnacht, but it doesn't go out of its way to make them feel welcome. Fasnacht is foremost for Baselers; it has remained a genuine folk celebration.

At least ten thousand people, a twentieth of the city's inhabitants, march in Fasnacht parades or perform in open-air skits regardless of the weather. Other tens of thousands line the streets and crowd the squares. During the months before carnival more than one hundred clubs, known as *cliques,* in various city neighborhoods have prepared masks and costumes, painted lanterns, and rehearsed sketches.

Starting in the dark at 4 A.M. on the Monday after Ash Wednesday, the *Morgenstreich* (morning stroke) opens the festivities. All the cliques parade to the center, many of the marchers blowing shrill piccolo flutes or lustily beating drums. Despite the ungodly hour, an astounding number of Baselers are on their feet to cheer the paraders. The marching and countermarching end in showers of confetti around 7 A.M., and many participants and onlookers repair to cafés and taverns to warm themselves with coffee, hot "meal soup" (a traditional Fasnacht treat), or something stronger.

In the afternoon the cliques stage more parades in the Marktplatz and other squares in the center. There is plenty of mummery, street theater, and spirited banter between masked Fasnacht characters and spectators. A visitor from abroad will have trouble grasping the meaning of many of the lampoons, which are traditionally aimed at local officials and personages, Swiss politicians, and world figures who have lately been in the news. The Basel vernacular reigns supreme. Members of the cliques taunt onlookers and are taunted back, all in the local dialect. The stranger can only grin instead of firing back a trenchant repartee.

The Tuesday of the Basel carnival is reserved for the children. Costumed and masked, they parade in the city center and in Lesser Basel, their proud parents among the onlookers. While this is going on, small bands of masked adults—members of the cliques or free-lance revelers— roam downtown neighborhoods. On Tuesday night many Fasnacht bands, the so-called Guggenmusik groups, playing traditional and improvised instruments, vie in Barfüsserplatz to produce the most discordant sounds.

On Wednesday the program is much the same as on
Monday, minus the predawn parade: more mummery,
skits, confetti, and caterwauling. Eventually the exhausted
affiliates of the cliques and other Baselers wind up in taverns to celebrate until the early hours of Thursday. Meanwhile the efficient sanitation department cleans the city of
confetti and other carnival debris. At 8 A.M. Thursday
Basel shows again its no-nonsense business face.

Fasnacht is preceded every January by a centuries-old
celebration in Lesser Basel, known as the day of the Vogel
Gryff (griffin). The mythical winged animal is the ancient
symbol of one of three right-bank neighborhood associations that go back to the Middle Ages, and which join
forces in the January rite.

The proceedings start on a day between January 13 and
27 with the "Wild Man," the symbol of another one of the
three groups, floating down the river in a boat. Wrapped in
leaves and carrying a small uprooted pine tree, he performs
rigidly prescribed dance steps in the boat, taking care never
to face the left bank—it's a Lesser Basel affair! Below the
Middle Bridge the "Wild Man," accompanied by drum-
mers, goes ashore on the right bank, ceremonially received
by the "Griffin" and by the "Lion," the symbol of the
third neighborhood association. The three costumed men
perform a grave dance and then parade through various
Lesser Basel neighborhoods. A formal banquet and another
parade round out the right-bank observance.

Exercise

Jogging. The promenades and parks on either side of the
Rhine—Schaffhauser Rheinweg with Solitude Park on the
right bank and St. Alban-Rheinweg with the gardens

flanking the mouth of the Birs River on the left bank—
offer plenty of space for jogging.

Swimming. The covered pool at Hallenbad Rialto, 45
Birsigstrasse (2819142), near the zoo, is a public facility.
It is open 9 A.M. to 9:30 P.M. Tuesday to Friday, and 10
A.M. to 5:30 P.M. Saturday and Sunday.

Public outdoor pools are as follows: Gartenbad Bach-
graben, 135 Belforterstrasse (434333), on the northwestern
outskirts (No. 6 tram from Barfüsserplatz and No. 38 bus);
Eglisee, 85 Egliseestrasse (6815300), on the northeastern
outskirts (No. 2 tram from SBB rail terminal); and St.
Jakob, 400 St. Jakobs-Strasse (3114144), near the soccer
stadium (No. 14 tram from Barfüsserplatz).

The public outdoor pools are generally open from the
beginning of May to the end of September. For information on public bathing establishments, call 3115010. Outdoor pools are also at the Basel Hilton (p. 106) and a few
other hotels.

There are two concessions for river bathing: Rheinbad
Breite, 195 St. Alban-Rheinweg (3112575), on the left
bank, upstream (No. 3 tram from Barfüsserplatz); and
Rheinbad St. Johann, St. Johanns-Rheinweg (3220442),
on the left bank downstream (No. 15 tram from Schifflände near the Middle Bridge).

Tennis. Public tennis courts at Sportanlage St. Jakob, 21
Brüglinger Strasse (3128896), near the soccer stadium (No.
14 tram). For other courts, inquire at Basler Lawn-Tennis
Club, Margarethenpark (2726941).

Golf. Basel golfers play at the eighteen-hole Geisberg
course near Hagenthal-le-Bas, Haut-Rhin (068-685091) in
France, a little more than 6 miles (10 kilometers) southwest

of the city. Inquire at Golf & Country Club Basel, 105 Horburg Strasse (6951111), in Lesser Basel.

Horseback riding. Reiterstadion Schänzli, Birsstrasse, Muttenz (3112241), is not quite 4 miles (6 kilometers) southeast of the city center. Reiterparadies, 16 Metzerlenstrasse, Mariastein (751506), is about 13 miles (20 kilometers) south of Basel.

Skiing. Beginners may prefer the nearby hills of the Black Forest in Germany or the French or Swiss Jura, but Baselers who take the sport seriously go by car or train to slopes in the Swiss Alps.

Ice-skating. Kunsteisbahn Margaretenpark (359595) is on the southern outskirts (No. 2 tram from the city center to the Margarethen stop, and No. 36 bus). Kunsteisbahn Eglisee is at 85 Egliseestrasse (6815300; see above, under "Swimming").

Spectator Sports

The dominant spectator sport is professional **soccer.** Important soccer matches are played in the St. Jakob Stadium (3124820), a part of the Basel sports center on the southeastern outskirts (No. 14 tram from Barfüsserplatz). For tickets to soccer events, contact Vorverkaufzenter Securitas, 43 Auf dem Wolf (3115353), near the stadium.

Emergencies

The **police emergency number** is 117. Police headquarters is at 6 and 12 Spiegelgasse, Spiegelhof (2677171), near Marktplatz.

The emergency number for the **fire department** is 118.

To summon an **ambulance,** call 144. The **emergency ward** of the Cantonal Hospital is at 2 Petersgraben (2652525), north of Marktplatz. For the various departments of the Cantonal Hospital, consult the telephone directory under *Kantonsspital*; for other hospitals and clinics, look under *Spitäler*.

Services

Most **post offices** are open 7:30 A.M. to noon and 1:30 to 6 P.M. Monday to Friday, 7:30 A.M. to 11 A.M. Saturday. Three major post offices are open 7:30 A.M. to 6:30 P.M. Monday to Friday: PTT Basel 1, 1 Rüdengasse, off Freie Strasse near Marktplatz; PTT Basel 2, Post-Passage, near the SBB rail terminal; and PTT Basel 5, 81 Claragraben, in Lesser Basel. Urgent matters are handled at a special window *(Dringlichkeitsschalter)* at PTT Basel 2; its hours are 6 to 7:30 A.M. and 6:30 to 10 P.M. Monday to Friday, 6 to 7:30 A.M. and 11 A.M. to 8 P.M. Saturday, and 9 A.M. to noon and 3 to 10 P.M. Sunday.

Banks are open 8:15 A.M. to 4:30 P.M. Monday to Wednesday and Friday, 8:15 A.M. to 5:30 P.M. Thursday. Exchange offices at the SBB rail terminal do business 6 A.M. to 10:15 P.M. daily, at the Baden Terminal 6:30 A.M. to 8:30 P.M. daily, at the EuroAirport Basel-Mulhouse, arrival and departure sections, 6:30 to 8:30 A.M. and 6 to 9 P.M. daily. An exchange office at the customs post on the motorway at the Swiss-German border near Weil is open 7 A.M. to 8 P.M. daily.

The **municipal and cantonal offices** are generally open 8 A.M. to noon and 2 to 5 P.M. Monday to Friday, but check beforehand; listings are in the Basel telephone directory under *Kant*.

Following is a list of additional services:

Alcoholics Anonymous. For an English-speaking group, call 2610453. The general information number is 753400.

Babysitters. Kinderhütedienst der Mütterhilfe, 158 Wasgenring (3028070), has listings of private babysitters.

Dentists. These are listed in the Basel telephone directory under *Zahnärzte*.

Lawyers. Listings of lawyers can be found in the Basel telephone directory under *Advokatur- und Notariatsbüros*.

Library. University Library, 18–20 Schönbeinstrasse (2673111), is near the Spalen Gate. It is open 8:30 A.M. to 7:30 P.M. Monday to Friday, and 8:30 A.M. to 4:30 P.M. Saturday.

Lost property. Inquire at Fundbüro, Basel Police Department, 12 Spiegelgasse (2677034), open 7:30 A.M. to noon and 1:30 to 4 P.M. Monday to Friday; Fundbüro, Basel Public Transport (BVB), 24 Barfüsserplatz (2678990), open 7:15 to 11:30 A.M. and 1:15 to 5:15 P.M. Monday to Friday; Swiss Federal Railways, Fundbüro SBB Terminal (2762467), open 7 A.M. to 7 P.M. daily.

Pharmacies. Pharmacies are listed in the Basel telephone directory under *Apotheken*. To find out which pharmacy has after-hours or night service on any given day, call 2611515.

Public toilets. These are in Basel's railroad terminals, in Marktplatz and some other squares, and in various public parks.

Religious services. For various Christian denominations, consult the Basel telephone directory under *Kirchen* and watch the announcements in the *Kirchenzettel* bulletins in the local newspapers on Friday and Saturday.

Protestant: Evangelical-Reformed Sunday service is held at the Münster (the Cathedral) in German at 10 A.M., in English and Spanish in the Münster's St. Nicholas Chapel (look for posted schedule).

Roman Catholic: Sunday masses are at 9 and 10:30 A.M. and 7 P.M.; Saturday mass is at 6:15 P.M. at Heiliggeist Kirche, 51 Thiersteiner Allee (3318088), on the southeastern outskirts (No. 16 tram from the city center).

Synagogues: Services are held daily in the newly restored double-domed building at 24 Leimenstrasse (2729170), built in 1868 and later enlarged, which has been designated a historic landmark.

Tourist information. Contact the Basel Tourist Board (Offizielles Verkehrsbüro Basel), 2 Blumenrain, CH-4001 Basel, Switzerland, phone (41-61) 2615050, fax (41-61) 2615944. It is open 8:30 A.M. to 6 P.M. Monday to Friday, and 8:30 A.M. to 1 P.M. Saturday.

Travel services. See listings in the Basel telephone directory under *Reisebüros*.

Shopping

Basel stores are open 8:30 A.M. to 6:30 P.M. Monday to Friday, and 8:30 A.M. to 5 P.M. Saturday; some are closed on Monday morning.

Department stores, large fashion shops, boutiques, and other retail businesses line Freie Strasse, cluster around Marktplatz, and are found in the central section of Lesser Basel. Many art galleries as well as antiques and old-book shops are in the up-and-down streets of the Spalen section, around the Civic Theater, in the St. Alban and Aeschen sections, and in side streets of Lesser Basel.

The leading department stores are Globus, in an art nouveau building at 2 Marktplatz (2615500), and Pfauen, 75 Freie Strasse (2616060), both on the left bank; and Jelmoli, 20 Rebgasse (681001), and Rheinbrücke, 22 Greifengasse (6959511), which are in Lesser Basel.

Two large apparel and fashion stores are C & A, 56 Freie Strasse (2619260), and Schild, 35 Freie Strasse (2612210).

At least 150 commercial art galleries are thriving in Basel. Best known internationally is Beyeler, 9 Bäumleingasse (2725412), near the Museum of Fine Arts.

For listings of other art galleries, look in the Basel telephone directory under *Galerien*. The telephone directory also lists antiques stores (under the heading *Antiquitäten*), old-book shops *(Antiquariate)*, and old and current coins *(Münzen)*.

Antiques and bric-a-brac are sold at an outdoor market in Münsterplatz in front of the Cathedral 9 A.M. to 4 P.M. every Saturday. A flea market *(Flohmärt)* is held in Marktplatz 1:30 to 6:30 P.M. on the second and fourth Wednesday of every month. Inexpensive clothing is sold in the square on the afternoons of the first and third Wednesday.

SIDE TRIPS

Visitors will enjoy paying a visit to the **"Swiss Pompeii."** Extensive ruins of the ancient Roman veterans' colony and town of Augusta Raurica that Lucius Munatius Plancus founded in 45–44 B.C. can be seen at Augst on the Rhine, 7.5 miles (12 kilometers) upstream from Basel. The modern town of **Kaiseraugst** (its name is a derivation from the German words for "Emperor Augustus") is a ten- to fifteen-minute walk from Augst and also contains Roman remains.

Frequent local trains from the Basel SBB rail terminal to Kaiseraugst take twelve minutes. The No. 70 bus from Aeschenplatz (halfway between the SBB rail terminal and the Rhine) to Kaiseraugst makes the trip in twenty-five minutes. From May to October boats of the Rhine Navigation Company sail from Schifflände near the Middle Bridge to Kaiseraugst in an hour and a half; return by boat or train. For information, call 2612400. The Basel Tourist Board conducts excursions with tour guides to Augst and Kaiseraugst by boat and rail every afternoon from May to October. The information number is 2615050.

Augst and Kaiseraugst are the vastest and best-preserved memorials to the presence of the ancient Romans in Switzerland. The military settlement that Plancus created eventually became a prosperous Roman town, which at its peak was home to twenty thousand people. Augusta Raurica was destroyed by Alemannic raiders in the late third century A.D., but the Roman military forces attempted to stem further barbaric invasions by building and garrisoning a large riverbank stronghold at what is now Kaiseraugst.

The Roman monuments of Augst include a theater from the second century A.D. that accommodated eight thousand spectators; a second-century temple opposite the theater at a spot where older sanctuaries once stood; and an amphitheater that was discovered in 1959. There are also the remains of the forum (marketplace), of a temple of Jupiter, of a curia (assembly building), and of a tavern with a large oven, unearthed in 1966. The restored basement of the curia contains an exhibition of Roman mosaics dug up in the area.

The Roman Museum and Roman House of Augst, 17 Giebenacher Strasse (8111187), near the Roman Theater, is open 10 A.M. to noon Tuesday to Sunday, and 1:30 to 6 P.M. (November to February: 5 P.M.) daily. Admission is $1.40, for adults, half price for children.

The museum stores 500,000 items excavated to date, but only a small number of them are on view in changing exhibitions. Most remarkable is a precious hoard of silver objects discovered in 1961 in the ancient fortress at Kaiseraugst (see below). The treasure, probably the property of a garrison commander, comprises sixty-eight pieces of a luxurious table service—ornamented plates, bowls, and spoons—in addition to a branched candlestick, a statuette of Venus, silver ingots, medallions, and coins.

The Roman House is a full-scale reconstruction, executed in 1955, of an ancient dwelling and business building of a type that was common when Augusta Raurica flourished. To be seen are a dining room with eating couches, marble tables, floor mosaics, and frescoed walls; a kitchen; a bath; and a workshop and salesroom—all equipped with objects found in the area or modern replicas of ancient models.

The remains in Kaiseraugst are impressive stretches of a fourth-century A.D. fortress wall and traces of an early-Christian baptistery, of vast public baths built toward the end of the third century A.D. and excavated as recently as 1974–76, and the kilns of a big tilery that were operated in the fourth century A.D. by Roman legions stationed on the empire's Rhine border.

In the warm months outdoor concerts and performances of classical drama take place occasionally in the Roman Theater of Augst. Watch the Basel newspapers and wall posters, or inquire at the Basel Tourist Board (2615050).

A good place for lunch or dinner in Augst is Rössli, 29 Hauptstrasse (8111016), an inn in a sixteenth-century building near the Roman Theater. Specialties are pike and other freshwater fish; full meals cost around $50 for two. Closed Monday and Tuesday. Guest rooms are also available.

Another interesting excursion is to the **Goetheanum at Dornach.** On a hillock at the foot of the Jura Mountains some 6 miles (10 kilometers) south of Basel, this large sculptured concrete building is the world center of the General Anthroposophical Society, founded by Rudolf Steiner (1861–1925). Theatrical and dance performances, lectures, and exhibitions are often held in it.

To reach the Goetheanum at 45 Rüttiweg (7014242, fax 7011160), take the yellow No. 10 regional tram from Aeschenplatz (halfway between the SBB rail terminal and the Rhine) to the last stop, Dornach Bahnhof. From the other side of the tracks walk along Bahnhofstrasse, turning left at Birseckweg, and follow the signs indicating the footpath to the Goetheanum.

Guided tours of the Goetheanum are conducted at 10 A.M. and 2:30 P.M. daily, except during meetings. For information, call 7014242. Vegetarian meals, coffee, and tea are available at the guesthouse, 2 Dorneckstrasse (7013372), below the Goetheanum.

The mighty concrete structure near Dornach was erected in 1924–28 according to Steiner's designs. It houses an Advanced School of Spiritual Science. Steiner, an Austrian philosopher and expert on the greatest German poet and writer, Johann Wolfgang von Goethe, taught anthroposophy (wisdom of humanity), the doctrine that humankind is the center of all spiritual endeavors.

Steiner's work and writings led to the creation of schools named after him in various parts of the world.

Basel, too, has a private Rudolf Steiner School, 54 Jakobs-
berger Holzweg (3316250), on the southeastern outskirts.

Portions from Goethe's *Faust* or, at times, the entire
immense two-part drama are staged at the Goetheanum
year after year. Works by Henrik Ibsen and contemporary
dramatists are also performed by the institution's own
troupe or by visiting companies, as well as occasional concerts, recitals, and ballets by local or guest artists and
groups. Watch Basel newspapers for Goetheanum programs. To reserve tickets, call 7014041, 9 A.M. to 12:30
P.M. and 3 to 6 P.M. Monday to Friday, and 9 A.M. to 12:30
P.M. Saturday.

Basel is a convenient starting point for additional day
trips. Two popular destinations are France's **Alsace region**
and the German state of **Baden-Württemberg.**

Mulhouse, with which Basel shares its airport, is an
industrial city and a culinary mecca. **Colmar,** north of
Mulhouse, is renowned for its Old Town with quaint
timber-framed houses and the celebrated Isenheim Altarpiece, a starkly realistic Crucifixion by Mathias Grünewald
(circa 1515), housed in Unterlinden Museum in a former
Dominican monastery.

The towns and little spas of Germany's **Black Forest**
hills are close to Basel. **Freiburg im Breisgau,** 40 miles
(65 kilometers) north of the Swiss city, is remarkable for
a Gothic cathedral with a 386-foot (117-meter) tower.

Passport and customs controls are normally breezy,
whether you travel by rail, bus, or private car. Basel's
Tourist Board (p. 141), the Swiss Federal Railways (information: 2726767), and private travel organizations arrange
guided tours and offer advice on individual trips to the two
neighboring countries.

4.

Geneva

GENEVA

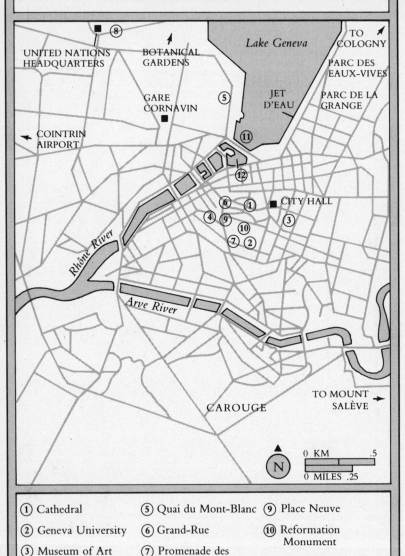

Lake Geneva

TO COLOGNY

UNITED NATIONS HEADQUARTERS

BOTANICAL GARDENS

PARC DES EAUX-VIVES

GARE CORNAVIN

JET D'EAU

PARC DE LA GRANGE

COINTRIN AIRPORT

Rhône River

CITY HALL

Arve River

TO MOUNT SALÈVE

CAROUGE

N

0 KM   .5
0 MILES   .25

① Cathedral

② Geneva University

③ Museum of Art and History

④ Grande Theatre

⑤ Quai du Mont-Blanc

⑥ Grand-Rue

⑦ Promenade des Bastions

⑧ Ariana Park

⑨ Place Neuve

⑩ Reformation Monument

⑪ Pont du Mont-Blanc

⑫ Rousseau Island

THE SCENIC, AFFLUENT city on the largest Alpine lake—Lake Geneva or, in French, Lac Léman—is to a remarkable extent international: its non-Swiss population accounts for fully one-third of its 165,000 residents. The French language as well as French civilization, manners, and cuisine nevertheless prevail in Geneva (French: Genève).

Geographically, the city is a near-enclave in France, attached to Switzerland by a corridor along the northern lakeshore that at a point near the Cointrin Airport narrows to 3 miles (4.8 kilometers).

Geneva houses the European headquarters of the United Nations and the central offices of some two hundred international bodies, from the Red Cross and the World Council of Churches to the European Center for Nuclear Research. International conferences, business conventions, and trade shows are often held in the city; such events bring battalions of diplomats, experts, technicians, secretaries, interpreters, security people, corporate execu-

tives, journalists—and possibly spies and adventurers—to
Geneva.

The broad sector of resident foreigners includes
wealthy expatriates who have happily adopted the French-
Swiss way of life, but also thousands of hotel and restaurant
workers from southern Europe and recent immigrants
from North Africa and Asia who make a living as laborers
and domestic workers or have started small businesses.
Furthermore, every working day thousands of persons
commute from nearby France to jobs in Geneva banks,
other offices, and stores.

English is widely understood and spoken in Geneva.
Natives today are more likely to speak English as their
second language than German, Italian, or Romansh, the
other official tongues of the Swiss Confederation. The idiom of Geneva, which Parisians amusedly call "Federal
French," has its particularities—like *septante*, *octante*, and
nonante for *soixante-dix* (seventy), *quatre-vingt* (eighty), and
quatre-vingt-dix (ninety)—and an unmistakable accent. Always tuned in to what is going on in France, the Genevois
(Genevans) will nevertheless emphasize that they are Swiss,
not French.

Actually, Geneva was a latecomer to the Swiss Confederation: the city with its hinterland of a few villages surrounded by French territory joined Switzerland only in
1815. Before that date there were many centuries of a
checkered history.

A settlement and trading post was established in pre-
Roman times at the strategic spot where the Rhône River
rushes out of Lake Geneva at 1,230 feet (375 meters) altitude above sea level. Julius Caesar passed through with his
legions in 58 B.C. and mentioned the place in his writings.

In the Middle Ages the city was for some time the
capital of the Kingdom of Burgundy, later defending itself

from expansionist neighbors, especially the dukes of Savoy.

Geneva's Old Town, an architectural gem with a Romanesque-Gothic cathedral and other stately buildings, attests to the city's wealth in the late Middle Ages and the Renaissance period. Geneva became a beacon of the Protestant Reformation during the sixteenth century, when the French theologian John Calvin sternly ruled it as a virtual theocracy for nearly three decades.

As an independent republic during the following centuries, Geneva became the refuge of French Protestants as well as of writers, intellectuals, and politicians who had been in trouble at home, like Voltaire. Annexed by Napoléon, Geneva was part of France for fifteen years until the Congress of Vienna, 1814–15, assigned the territory to Switzerland.

The crescent-shaped Lake Geneva, 45 miles (73 kilometers) long and 2 to 9 miles (3.2 to 14.5 kilometers) wide, confers on the city a sense of spaciousness and opens magnificent vistas. Its western tip and the Rhône bisect Geneva. On clear days the northern lakeshore commands a panorama of the glaciers and snowy ridges of Europe's loftiest mountain massif, the Mont Blanc. Geneva is proud of its vast, lovingly nursed public gardens; there are at least three trees and one hundred flowers for every resident within the city limits.

The best time to visit Geneva is from May to October. In summer the temperature seldom reaches or exceeds 86 degrees Fahrenheit (30 centigrade). With its crowded café terraces, elegant lakeside promenades, white excursion boats, and swarms of yachts in the lake, the luminous ambiance is that of a fashionable resort. The city also has much to offer in the cold months when the *bise*, an icy north wind, sweeps across the lake. Snow is rare. There are smart shops, fine restaurants, art exhibitions and auctions, renowned museums, and a vigorous musical and theatrical life.

ARRIVAL AND DEPARTURE

Geneva's smoothly functioning **Cointrin Airport** is only 2.5 miles (4 kilometers) from downtown and is linked with the city's railroad terminal, Gare Cornavin, by frequent trains. Passport and customs formalities are the same as in Zurich (p. 25). Only a few steps to the left of the arrivals building is the railroad station from which trains depart every ten to fifteen minutes from early morning to late at night. Most trains proceed to Lausanne, other cities in Switzerland, or to Italy after stopping in the Geneva terminal (Gare Cornavin).

The rail trip from the airport to the Cornavin terminal, which is close to the center of Geneva, takes six minutes and costs $2.70 in second class, around $4.20 in first. There is always plenty of space in second-class coaches. Cabs are plentiful at the airport; a taxi ride to Geneva's center will be around $20. Coaches for Swiss lakeside towns and destinations in the nearby regions of France leave from the airport at short intervals. Several car-rental firms operate from the airport building.

Glittering watch and jewelry shops are conspicuous among the concessions in the airport lounge. Post offices, bank branches, and money exchanges will be found in the arrivals and departures sections; there are also restaurants, coffee shops, newsstands, souvenir shops, a large duty-free store, and a pharmacy.

For flight information, call 7993111; airport management, 7177111; railroad terminal at the airport (Gare Genève-Aéroport), 7910250.

The busy Geneva railroad terminal, **Gare Cornavin,** is one-third of a mile (about half a kilometer) from the lake's north shore. The straight, broad Rue du Mont-Blanc leads from the lakefront up to the Place Cornavin, with direct access to the vast underground shopping mall adjacent to the rail terminal.

The Cornavin terminal handles EuroCity and other international trains to and from Spain, France, Italy, and Germany, in addition to many InterCity trains to and from Swiss centers, and local traffic. TGVs (*trains à grande vitesse,* ultrafast trains) of the French National Railways (SNCF) link Geneva with Paris at various times every day. The TGVs cover the nearly 320 miles (520 kilometers) between the two cities in three and a half hours. Seat reservations in first and second class are obligatory. The French National Railways have a special ticket office (7316450) at the Cornavin terminal.

The Cornavin terminal telephone number for train information is 7316450; for other services and lost property, call 7152111. The official Geneva Tourist Office is in the terminal building (7385200), open 9 A.M. to 6 P.M. Monday to Saturday.

Motorists arrive in Geneva from Zurich, Bern, Basel, and Lausanne on Motor Road N-1 by the Rue de Lausanne along the northwestern lakeshore, or by way of the Cointrin Airport; from Paris on N-1 past the airport; from Milan on Motor Road N-9 through the upper Rhône Valley to Lausanne and by N-1; and from southern France and northwestern Italy (by way of the Mont Blanc tunnel) on the French Motor Road A-40 with exits leading into Geneva's southern suburbs.

For assistance in a mechanical breakdown on the road, call Secours Routier, 140. For other assistance, motorists should contact Touring-Club Suisse, 9 Rue Pierre-Fatio (7371212, emergency number 7358000), near the southern lakeshore, or Automobile-Club de Suisse, 21 Rue Fontenette (422233), in the Carouge section on Geneva's southwestern outskirts.

TRANSPORTATION

An efficient network of tramcars, trolley cars, and buses covers the city and its suburbs. Tickets must be bought from the vending machines at the stops; the machines carry system maps. Fares are $1.40 for short trips (up to three stops) and $1.70 for longer trips with unlimited transfers during one hour. Children between the ages of six and sixteen pay 85¢. All-day network passes at $4.70 are available at the Transports Publics Genevois (TPG) window in the underground mall close to the Cornavin terminal.

Taxi ranks are outside the Cornavin terminal and near major hotels. For radio-dispatched cabs, call 141. Taxis charge $3.85 on entry and $1.60 for each additional kilometer (about three-fifths of a mile); there are extra fees for late-hour and holiday services. For cabs outside the Central Taxi-Phone (141) system—they may charge lower or higher fares—consult the Geneva telephone directory under *Taxis*; for limousine services, under *Automobiles, location d'*.

A sightseeing bus with an English-speaking guide leaves from the bus terminal, Place Dorcière (7320230), near the Quai du Mont-Blanc on the lake's north shore, at 2 P.M. daily, from April to October at 10 A.M. daily. The fare for the two-hour tour is $15.

Sightseeing boats sail from the docks on the Quai du Mont-Blanc daily from the beginning of March to the end of October. Watch the billboards along the Quai du Mont-Blanc, or call Swissboat, 7324747; Compagnie Générale de Navigation, 3212521; or Mouettes Genevoises, 7322944. For the Cruise of Famous Residences, see p. 209. *Mouettes* (sea gulls) are motorboats that ferry passengers across the lake in about five minutes and call at various parks and other points along the northern and southern lakeshores.

ACCOMMODATIONS

It is characteristic of opulent Geneva that two-thirds of its thirteen thousand hotel beds are in deluxe or first-class houses (five or four stars). Visitors who want to stay in a less expensive place should make reservations well ahead of their scheduled arrival, especially if they plan to visit the International Motor Show in spring or some other event that usually fills up hotels in the city and its vicinity. During international conventions or trade shows some participants and visitors put up in cities as distant as Lausanne or Fribourg and commute to Geneva. Whenever diplomatic conferences are held in Geneva, it is easier to find a room in some modest hotel than in any of the top-rated establishments.

Travelers arriving in Geneva without a hotel reservation may want to consult the electronic signboard at the Cornavin terminal (ground floor, opposite the Tourist Information Office); it indicates which houses in the various price brackets have vacant rooms. A toll-free telephone links visitors directly with the reception desk of the selected hotel.

Breakfast is included in the room rates of all five-star

hotels and in those of most other houses. Travel agents, tour operators, and travel managers of large corporations are aware of so-called confidential hotel rates for travel groups and corporate rates for business clients. Ask your travel agent or inquire at the Geneva Tourist Information Office about weekend packages and other cut-rate arrangements.

Following is a list of recommended hotels, grouped according to the official categories. Other houses would also qualify for inclusion and are left out for reasons of space.

Five-star Houses ($300 to $500 for a double room)

Eight of Geneva's sixteen top-rated hotels are on the lake-front or on the Rhône. The outstanding establishments are:

Beau-Rivage, 13 Quai du Mont-Blanc (7310221, fax 7387551), has been in business for more than a hundred years. Owned and managed by the Mayer hotel dynasty, the hotel cites among its former guests the Duke of Windsor before he became King Edward VIII, other royalty, General Charles de Gaulle, Charlie Chaplin, and any number of Astors, Rockefellers, and Indian maharajas. In the elegant, curving salon of Suite 119/20, a picture of a youthful "Sissi" is a reminder of the beautiful Empress Elisabeth of Austria-Hungary, who died there in 1898 shortly after being stabbed by a twenty-four-year-old Italian anarchist (p. 181).

The 120-room house with its glamorous, romantic, and tragic reminiscences has superb service and an excellent restaurant.

Le Richemond, near the foregoing hotel, at Jardin Brunswick, 8–10 Rue Adhémar-Fabri (7311400, fax 7316709), is slightly off the lakefront but has a lake view. Owned since 1875 by the Armleder family, it is the traditional rival of the Beau-Rivage, a little more expensive, with a wealthy and devoted international clientele. There are ninety-seven rooms and a glitzy restaurant.

Des Bergues, 33 Quai des Bergues (7315050, fax 7321989), overlooks the extreme tip of the lake where it releases the Rhône River, and faces the Rousseau Islet. The old and quietly elegant house has a predominantly French-speaking clientele and is favored by Swiss politicians and business executives. Its bar is a meeting place for bankers, financiers, and corporate leaders.

Noga Hilton, 19 Quai du Mont-Blanc (7319811, fax 7386432), is a modern lakefront establishment that has recently been further enlarged so as to become Geneva's largest five-star house (593 beds). It has a shopping arcade, a heated swimming pool, two nightclubs, and good restaurants. Adjacent is a theater where pop stars and rock groups often perform and where plays are occasionally staged. The same building complex houses Geneva's only gambling casino (p. 197). Wealthy Middle Eastern and Japanese visitors to Geneva tend to flock to this hotel.

InterContinental, 7–9 Petit Saconnex (7346091, fax 7342864), near the United Nations Palace and the headquarters of other international organizations, is a modern high rise. It is favored by diplomats, oilmen, high business executives, and journalists. The telephones in the 320 rooms and suites have sockets for computer modems and fax machines. International conferences are frequently held in its meeting rooms. Other amenities include a swimming pool and a fitness club.

Métropole, 34 Quai du Général-Guisan (3111344, fax

3111350), on the southern lakefront, is a distinguished older house with a fine view of the lake and the parks. The room rates are at the lower end of the five-star range.

Les Armures, 1 Puits-Saint-Pierre (3109172, fax 3109846), in the Old Town, is a quiet luxury hotel in a Renaissance building on a charming little square close to the Cathedral, with only fifty-two beds. Art traders and collectors like it.

La Réserve, 301 Route de Lausanne (7741741, fax 7742571), is near the northern lakeshore in the suburb of Bellevue, not quite 4 miles (6 kilometers) from downtown Geneva. This is a ranch-style resort hotel in a vast garden, with 114 rooms and suites, indoor and outdoor pools, tennis courts, and a fitness club. Its restaurants include the renowned Tsé-Fung (p. 167).

Four-star Hotels ($160 to $335 for a double room)

Angleterre, 17 Quai du Mont-Blanc (7328180, fax 7386286), is a corner building on the lakefront with sixty-five rooms (ten suites), good service, and a faithful clientele.

Tiffany, 18 Rue de l'Arquebuse (3293311, fax 3208991), in a quiet neighborhood on the left bank of the Rhône, opened in 1990 in a turn-of-the-century building and has only thirty-seven beds.

Ambassador, 21 Quai des Bergues (7317200, fax 7389080), in a central location on the right bank of the Rhône, overlooks the busy Rue Rousseau and faces the Old Town across the river.

De Berne, 26 Rue de Berne (7316000, fax 7311173), is

near the Cornavin rail terminal. A modern house with good service.

Warwick, 14 Rue de Lausanne (7316250, fax 7389935), faces the rail terminal. This large modern establishment has conference and banquet rooms and a fitness club. Business clientele.

La Cicogne, 17 Place Longuemalle (3114242, fax 3114065), is near the southern lakefront, in the main shopping district. This house is not officially classified because it doesn't belong to the Swiss Hotel Association, but it would qualify for at least four-star status. Once a place with a shady reputation, the building was completely restructured and refurbished in the 1980s. Each of its fifty rooms and suites, with soundproof windows, is decorated and furnished in a different style, from Old French to art nouveau.

Three-star Hotels ($85 to $145 for a double room with private bath)

Suisse, 10 Place Cornavin (7326630, fax 7326329), faces the rail terminal. No restaurant.

Mon-Repos, 131 Rue de Lausanne (7328010, fax 7328595), near the United Nations Palace (No. 4 bus to the Sécheron stop), is comfortable, with balconies, a flowery terrace, and a good restaurant. Also furnished apartments.

Astoria, 6 Place Cornavin (7321025, fax 7317690), near the rail terminal, has nice rooms. No restaurant.

Windsor, 31 Rue de Berne (7317130, fax 7319325), is near the rail terminal. Single rooms without private bath, $60. No restaurant.

International et Terminus, 20 Rue des Alpes (7328095, fax 7321843), is an older house near the rail terminal. Singles without private bath, $55; doubles without private bath, $75.

Two-star Selections

Lido, 8 Rue de Chantepoulet (7315530, fax 7316501), is near the Cornavin terminal. A family-run house with sixty beds; plain but well kept and friendly. Reserve early. Double rooms with bath or shower, $85. No restaurant.

Luserna, 12 Avenue Luserna (3441600, fax 3444936), located on the northwestern outskirts (No. 10 bus to the Servette stop). A fifty-eight-bed house in a garden; very quiet. Double rooms without private bath and without breakfast, $70; with bath and breakfast, around $90.

Pax, 68 Rue du 31-Décembre (7354440, fax 7864668), near the southern lakeshore, central location. Double rooms without private bath and without breakfast, $75; with bath and breakfast, $95. No restaurant.

Apartment Hotels and Apartment Houses

A number of real estate companies rent furnished studios and apartments, usually with fully equipped kitchenettes, to the many members of international organizations stationed in Geneva and to visitors who stay for at least a month. Listings are in the Geneva telephone directory under *Appartements et studios meublés* and *Résidences*.

Inspect the premises thoroughly and make sure there are no pending telephone or utilities bills before committing yourself. A refundable deposit is customary. For real estate agents, consult the Geneva telephone directory under

Agences immobilières. Also scan the classified ads for apartments and houses in the local newspapers.

Youth Hostel and Youth Accommodations

Nouvelle Auberge de Jeunesse, 28–30 Rue Rothschild (7326260), is near the northern lakefront (Quai Wilson). It has 350 beds and bunk beds for men and women. The membership card of the International Federation of Youth Hostels is required. Guests may cook their own meals. Open all year.

Foyer l'Accueil, 8 Rue Alcide-Jentzer (3209277), is on the city's southern outskirts. It has 104 beds for women only.

Armée du Salut (Salvation Army), 14 Rue de l'Industrie (7336438), is on the southern outskirts. It has thirty beds for women only. Inexpensive warm meals are served at lunch- and dinnertime.

Camping Sites

Sylvabelle, 10 Chemin de Conches (3470603), on the northeastern outskirts, nearly 2 miles (3 kilometers) from the city center (No. 8 bus), has bungalows. Open April to October.

Pointe-à-la-Bise—TCS, Vesenaz (7521296), is on the eastern outskirts, 4.5 miles (7 kilometers) from the city center (E bus). Operated by the Swiss Touring Club. Open April to September.

Camping d'Hermance, Chemin de Glerrets, Hermance (7511483), is on the eastern outskirts, 9 miles (14 kilometers) from the city center (E bus).

EATING OUT

Geneva's cooking and eating habits are close to those of
neighboring France but are also influenced by the dishes of
Switzerland's other French-speaking cantons and even by
the Alemannic, Alsatian, and Italian cuisines. The main
meal of the day is lunch; many stores, offices, and workshops give their staffs a midday break of ninety minutes to
two hours. For most Genevois, dinner is a lighter affair
around 8 P.M. After 9:30 P.M. it's hard to get a warm meal
in many of the simpler eating places. This does not apply
to the more elaborate restaurants patronized by expense-
account guests and by the many foreign residents and visitors.

Dishes typical of the restaurants, cafés, and brasseries
in Lyon, which is only 100 miles (160 kilometers) to the
west, and in Paris may also be found on Genevan menus:
from *soupe à l'oignon* (onion soup) to *bifteck frites* (steak with
french fries) to Alsatian-type *choucroûte garnie* (ham, lard,
sausages, and sauerkraut).

In addition, Geneva is an excellent place for sampling
the culinary specialties of *la Suisse romande* (French-
language Switzerland). Foremost among them is fondue in
its various versions.

Fondue is French for *molten* or *blended*. The cheese-based
dish, originally a frugal staple food of the region around
Neuchâtel, is a classic in the *carnotzets*—cozy, wood-
paneled taverns—but is also served in many cafés and restaurants.

Authentic fondue is prepared in a broad earthenware
pot, called *caquelon*, which is lightly rubbed with garlic and
filled with dry white wine. A little lemon juice is added.
While the wine is slowly heated over an open flame,
coarsely grated Emmenthal or Gruyère cheese is gradually

stirred in with a wooden spoon. When bubbles rise to the surface and a homey smell wafts through the room, some kirsch is poured into the brew. For spiciness, a little pepper or grated nutmeg may also be sprinkled in. Meanwhile, one-inch bread cubes have been heaped on a platter; French bread that isn't too fresh and won't easily crumble is traditional (the crust is not cut off).

To enjoy fondue properly, one spears a cube with a long fork, dips it into the pot, moves it around—a figure-eight pattern is recommended—so that it gets a thick coat, and eats the morsel. The heat, possibly from a spirit burner, stays on but is regulated so the shrinking contents of the bowl simmer without ever boiling.

It isn't necessary to wash down the mildly alcoholic fondue with any beverage. Cold beer, chilled soft drinks, or cold water at any rate are out because, as the Swiss will warn you, they would upset the fondue eater's stomach. Instead, a glass of the same wine that went into the pot or perhaps two fingers of kirsch in a tumbler are appropriate. The customary shot of kirsch halfway through a fondue meal is called the *coup de milieu*.

The wines grown on the chalky soils of the Auvernier, Boudry, and Colombier vineyards near Neuchâtel are naturals for fondue; but Fendant from the Canton Valais or indeed any dry white wine will do.

Fondue asks for company: four to six persons around the table are the ideal numbers. In Switzerland the rule is that anyone who lets a bread cube slip from the fork into the fondue has to buy a bottle of wine. Your chances of avoiding such a penalty improve if you seek out cubes with a crust.

Fondue Bourguignonne, named after France's Burgundy region, substitutes beef for cheese. A metal pot is nearly filled with olive oil or stock and heated to boiling. One-inch cubes of lean beef fillet are heaped on a platter. Each guest spears a cube and dips it into the bowl until the meat is done to taste. Before eating it, one dips the cube into one of several seasonings and sauces—various mustards, Worcestershire sauce, paprika—arrayed in cups and plates on the table. Salt, pepper, onion rings, pickles, and olives should also be on hand.

Chinese fondue, a newcomer, is offered by several Genevan cafés. Razor-thin slices of meat are dipped into a pot of boiling stock. When all meat is eaten, the broth, which has become a rich soup, is drunk out of cups.

Dessert fondues are made with grated milk chocolate, cream, eggs, fruit jelly, or honey. Cookies or marshmallows are dipped into the sweet concoction. Confectioners occasionally offer the dessert, but for the richest flavor one has to be invited to a celebration with children in a Genevan home.

The other standby of the *carnotzets* is raclette, a cheese dish that originated in the Canton Valais but has become a favorite in Geneva. The name raclette is derived from the French verb *racler* (to scrape). The fat cheese made of unskimmed Alpine milk from the Bagnes Valley, northeast of the Great St. Bernard Pass, is preferred for the dish, but some sorts of Gruyère are used as well. If prepared over a charcoal or log fire, the dish gains the smoky flavor that connoisseurs relish, but it's hard to find such Alpine authenticity in Geneva. In the city, electric-heating elements specially designed for raclette are generally employed.

The mountain rituals are always observed: The chef or waiter cuts a wheel of cheese, large as a pumpkin, in two and pares the rind at the top of one of the halves so that a fatty, golden strip emerges. The flat part of the half-moon cheese is held to the source of heat. When the surface starts curling, the top layer is quickly scraped off with a long knife and put on a plate. The maneuver is repeated until a sizable helping has been assembled, and then maybe another plate is filled.

Raclette is customarily served with boiled potatoes in their skins and small, pickled onions. The cheese scrapings must never be cut with a knife and should be eaten while still hot. Fendant wine is the correct accompaniment; as with fondue, drinking beer or other cold beverages is an unspeakable gaffe. Raclette places usually offer the dish *à volonté*—eat as much as you can handle.

Other frequent listings on Genevan restaurant menus are, despite their French names, Alemannic-Swiss: *viande des Grisons* is *Bündnerfleisch* (raw, smoked-dried beef, finely sliced) and *émincé de veau* is *Geschnetzeltes* (minced and creamed veal in a usually bland sauce). Lake fish, mostly perch, is often served filleted and fried or browned in butter. Higher-class Geneva restaurants offer fresh seafood flown in daily from France. There is an abundance of sausage. Pizza seems ubiquitous, as is Italian-style espresso (spelled *expresso* and pronounced with the stress on the last syllable). The more than one thousand eating and drinking places in Geneva include many British-style pubs as well as Hispanic, Asian, and North African restaurants.

The carafe wines often come from the nearby hillside: Perlan is Geneva's popular white wine, Gamay is red. Among the open wines available in most restaurants are white Fendant, red Goron, and Dôle from the Valais, as well as the vintages from the Lausanne and Neuchâtel areas.

International gourmets and food critics agree that the best restaurants of Geneva and its environs are on a par with top-rated establishments in Paris, Lyon, and other shrines of French cuisine. The rule of thumb of discriminat-

ing travelers to shun hotel meals doesn't apply to the five-
star houses in Geneva; quite a few of them boast excellent
restaurants.

Top Restaurants

Hôtel de Ville, better known as **Chez Girardet,** 1 Rue
d'Yverdon, 1023 Crissier (021-6340505), is some 40 miles
(63 kilometers) northeast of Geneva and not quite 2 miles
(3 kilometers) northwest of Lausanne. Some well-heeled
epicures who have made reservations months ahead go on
a gastronomic pilgrimage from Geneva to this establishment, owned by Freddy Girardet. It is widely praised as
the best restaurant in Switzerland and one of the best in all
of Europe. Count on $150 to $200 a person for dinner,
with wine.

Le Béarn, 4 Quai de la Poste (3110028), on the left bank
of the Rhône, is an intimate place with French Empire
decor. Bankers entertain important clients here, treating
them to lobster or foie gras. Also oysters, roast game in
season, fine pastry. Closed for lunch Saturday and all Sunday. Dinner around $120 a person.

Le Cygne, 19 Quai du Mont-Blanc (7319811), is the second-floor restaurant of the Noga Hilton (p. 157), with a
lake view. French-oriented cuisine, with daily fresh seafood, and remarkable service. Dinner with a bottle from
the impressive wine list may run as much as $110 to $130
a person.

Le Gentilhomme, 8–10 Rue Adhémar-Fabri (7311400),
the restaurant of the hotel Le Richemond (p. 156), stuns
by its opulent decor. French cooking with an accent on
lighter dishes. About $100 a person.

Le Chat Botté, 13 Quai du Mont-Blanc (7316532), on

the ground floor of the hotel Beau-Rivage (p. 156), with a terrace, cultivates classic French cuisine. $100 to $120 a person.

Parc des Eaux-Vives, 82 Quai Gustave-Ador (7354140), in a splendid garden on the lake's south bank, offers a friendly welcome, impeccable service, and such traditional French dishes as frog legs and *poulet de Bresse* as well as fresh seafood. Closed for dinner Sunday and all Monday.

Perle du Lac, 128 Rue de Lausanne (7317935), is a luxury restaurant in the Perle du Lac estate favored by diplomats.

Auberge du Lion d'Or, 5 Place Pierre-Gautier, Cologny (7364432), in an elegant suburb on the lake's southern shore, is a ten-minute cab ride from the center of Geneva. It has a terrace overlooking the lake and the city, and is famous for fresh lake fish, superb desserts, and an ample wine cellar. The check for two may run to $250.

Tsé-Fung, 301 Route de Lausanne (7741741), on the lake's north shore, in the hotel La Réserve (p. 158), is reputed to be Switzerland's finest Chinese restaurant. International financiers are frequent patrons. The decor is in red and black, the cuisine Szechuan-inspired. Unlike most Chinese eating places, Tsé-Fung has a vast wine list with rare French vintages. Dinner for two, about $200.

Honorable mention: the French-oriented restaurants of the hotels **Des Bergues** (p. 157) and **InterContinental** (p. 157).

Other Outstanding Eating Places

Les Armures, 1 Rue du Puits-Saint-Pierre (3103442), near the Cathedral, claims to be Geneva's oldest bistro and *car-*

notzet. The restaurant with rooms on various levels is snug, though a tad touristy. It serves *choucroûte garnie,* fondue, pizza, cold cuts, and other snacks as well as oysters flown in from France. A full meal with some wine or beer needn't cost more than $50 to $60 a person.

Brasserie Lipp, 8 Rue de la Confédération (3293122), on the third floor of the elegant, multilevel Confédération Centre shopping mall, is an offshoot of the famous Parisian left-bank establishment and a trendy place for light lunches and dinners. The classic Alsatian dish *choucroûte garnie* (small, medium size, and large) and sausages dominate the menu; also quiche and other snacks. A full meal runs $30 to $40 a person. Open daily until at least midnight.

Café-Restaurant Brasserie Landoldt, 2 Rue Candolle (3290536), near the Grand Théâtre, is an old establishment for coffee, lunch, snacks, and pre-opera dinners. Long popular with the Geneva intelligentsia (Lenin fancied it), it is now managed by the Mövenpick chain.

Brasserie de la Bourse, 7 Place du Marché, Carouge (3420466), is located at the center of the ex-Piemontese Carouge section.

Comparatively Inexpensive

Café de Paris, 26 Rue du Mont-Blanc (7328450), is near the Cornavin rail terminal. It is renowned for its standard $23 entrecôte with herb butter on top, french fries, and green salad. Open wines.

Chez Bouby, 1 Rue Grenus (7310927), is near the right bank of the Rhône, in the city center. This is the typical bistro with snacks and meals; open wines. Full dinner is around $35 a person.

Kosher Food

Shalom, 78 Rue du Rhône (3289093), central location. Closed Friday night and Saturday.

Self-Service and Fast Food

Manora, 6 Rue Cornavin (7313146), with access from the street near the Cornavin rail terminal and from the Placette department store, is a big, bustling cafeteria with a large selection of salads, a few options for warm food, and a spread of desserts and fruits; wine, beer, and soft drinks are available. $10 to $15 will buy a filling meal. Open daily.

MIGROS, the vast cooperative, has branches at 1–2 Place des Charmilles (344550), in the city's west, near the right bank of the Rhône, and elsewhere. Consult the Geneva telephone directory under *Migros*. Closed Sunday.

McDonald's, 22 Rue du Mont-Blanc (7329718), near the Cornavin rail terminal; 4 Cours-de-Rive (3218575), central location. Both open daily.

Pizza Hut, 22 Place Cornavin (7380822), near the rail terminal. Open daily.

Wendy's, 42 Rue du Rhône (3295050), central location. Open daily.

Coffee and Chocolate

Du Rhône Chocolatier, 3 Rue de la Confédération (3115614), central location, offers coffee, tea, or hot chocolate on the premises and excellent chocolates to take out.

Teuscher, 8 Rue de la Confédération (3104410), in the

Confédération Centre mall, is the shop of a renowned chocolate firm.

La Clémence, 20 Place du Bourg-de-Four (3201096), is on a small square a few steps east of the Cathedral, with an outdoor terrace. Genevans start coming here as students and nostalgically return in later life. Coffee and snacks, but the ambiance is the main asset.

Rusterholz, 13 Rue de la Cité (3114604), at the lower approaches to the Old Town, is an old-fashioned tearoom and *confiserie* with good coffee and fresh pastry as well as light lunches.

Picnic Food

Buy bread, sandwiches, cold cuts, cheeses, fruits, and beverages at one of the shops in the underground mall in front of the Cornavin rail terminal, or in one of the several outlets of the MIGROS cooperative (see telephone directory), or in the food court of the Placette department store, 9 Rue Grenus (7317400), not far from the rail terminal.

WHAT TO SEE

The core of Geneva is one of the best-preserved and most architecturally harmonious urban neighborhoods from the Middle Ages to the baroque era in all of Europe. At the foot of the Old Town the main financial and shopping districts of the modern city stretch out on the south shore of the lake and the left bank of the Rhône. The right bank of the river is taken up by a business section, and the northern lakefront by big hotels and other stately buildings. The United Nations Palace and the headquarters of other international bodies cluster amid parks and greenery on the northern outskirts.

Central Geneva seems to be made for strolling. Its sights can be conveniently visited on foot. For an audio-guided individual tour of the Old Town, contact the Geneva Tourist Information Office at the Cornavin rail terminal (7385200); this office rents tape recorders with a cassette that gives a running commentary in English or other major languages on twenty-six points of interest. The rental fee is about $7.50; a $37 deposit is refundable. For walking tours with a guide, inquire at the Tourist Information Office. For the daily sightseeing coach, see p. 154.

The Old Town

The ancient nucleus of the city occupies a hill with the eight-hundred-year-old Cathedral at its top. A good start-ing point for a stroll up the slope is the busy **Place Bel-Air** on the left bank of the Rhône, the bridgehead of the Pont de l'Ile, the fourth passage across the river counting from the tip of the lake. Several tram- and bus lines con-verge on the square. Walk past imposing bank palaces to the Rue de la Cité, which starts steeply and leads straight to the **Grand-Rue,** the gently rising main street of old Geneva. It is today lined with commercial art galleries, old-book shops, cafés, and taverns on the ground floors and in the basements of dignified old buildings.

At No. 11 Grand-Rue is the mansion in which those holding the post of resident of France were ensconced for two hundred years until 1794. A kind of superambass-ador of the French king, the resident was supposed to make sure that the nominally independent Republic of Geneva did nothing against the interests of the powerful French monarch.

A side street, **Rue de la Pélisserie,** opens a few steps farther up, on the left. A plaque at No. 82 Rue de la Pélisserie records that the English novelist George Eliot (Mary Ann Evans) lived in the house from 1849 to 1850.

The restored facade of the house at No. 40 Grand-Rue carries a plaque in memory of the birth in it, in 1712, of Geneva's most illustrious son, Jean-Jacques Rousseau. The immensely influential philosopher and writer had an often troubled relationship with his native city and at one time was exiled by it. Rousseau spent many years in France and died there in 1778.

The Grand-Rue ends at an arcaded structure from the sixteenth century, the **Arsenal,** originally a granary. The open street-floor hall contains five of the many artillery pieces that were once placed on Geneva's ramparts. Now children of visiting school classes are often seen clambering onto the old guns.

The facades of the Arsenal are adorned with a sundial, the coat of arms of Geneva, and nineteenth-century frescoes depicting scenes from the city's history. On the inner walls of the hall of guns are three mosaics that were made in 1950; these mosaics also recall episodes from Geneva's past, including the arrival of Julius Caesar in 58 B.C.

A part of the Arsenal building today houses **the city's archives,** containing, among many other historical documents, some papers in Calvin's handwriting.

A few steps to the left of the Arsenal, at 6 Rue du Puits-Saint-Pierre, is the **Maison Tavel,** said to be Geneva's oldest dwelling, at present a remarkable museum (p. 188).

To the right of the Arsenal, at 2-4 Rue de l'Hôtel-de-Ville, is Geneva's massive **City Hall,** built between the fifteenth and the seventeenth centuries. The edifice contains meeting halls and offices of the cantonal and municipal governments.

Entering the courtyard from No. 2, the visitor sees a cobbled ramp that permitted city worthies to reach the upper floors on horseback or in a litter.

Ask the concierge at the entrance if you want to see the so-called Alabama Hall across the courtyard. (A tip of a couple of francs per person is in order.) Two historic events occurred in the hall. On August 22, 1864, the international treaty establishing the Red Cross Organization for the alleviation of human suffering was signed in it. In 1871–72 a five-man international arbitration tribunal met here to settle a conflict between the United States and Britain that had arisen from British shipyards furnishing the Confederate Navy with the raider *Alabama* and other cruisers during the War between the States. Naval paraphernalia is displayed in the hall.

From City Hall a short street and a little square with eighteenth-century houses, **the Taconnerie,** lead to the **Cathedral of St. Peter.** The great edifice is a mixture of Romanesque, Gothic, and neoclassical styles. It was started in the twelfth century, was in part rebuilt four hundred years later, and received the addition of an incongruous Greco-Roman portico at its main entrance in the eighteenth century. A vast project for the consolidation and restoration got under way in the 1970s.

The Cathedral rises at a spot where a Christian church was built toward the end of the Roman Empire, in the fifth century A.D. Other Christian sanctuaries and a baptistery with its own water well were erected nearby in the early Middle Ages.

Systematic exploration of the subsoil below and near the Cathedral started in 1973 and is continuing. Archeologists have so far discovered the remains of early-Christian sanctuaries, a bishop's palace, and attached buildings— a veritable underground city. Remarkable mosaics with intricate geometrical patterns, once forming the pavements of some halls, have also come to light.

The archeological site beneath the Cathedral can be visited; access is over a stairway at the right side of the main entrance to St. Peter's. The site is open 10 A.M. to 1 P.M. and 2 to 6 P.M. Tuesday to Sunday. Guided tours are conducted at 8:30 P.M. on some Thursdays and 6 P.M. on some Saturdays. Admission is $3.75 for adults, $2.30 for children. Cassettes and tape recorders for audio-guided individual tours can be rented.

The Cathedral is flanked by two square Gothic towers. The visitor may ascend the north tower (access from the church's interior, see below); the south tower has been under repair for years. The tall spire between the towers is from 1895.

The interior of the Cathedral breathes the austere spirit of the Reformation. After centuries of Roman Catholic worship in the large building, the Protestant Reformation movement had conquered Geneva in 1536, and its followers stripped the edifice of images of the saints and ornaments. John Calvin had meanwhile arrived in the city, was elected preacher in 1537, and started expounding his doctrines from the pulpit. After a few years' banishment from Geneva he returned triumphantly in 1541, resumed his teachings, wrote theological treatises, and corresponded with Reformation leaders all over Europe, thus making Geneva the "Protestant Rome." He also involved himself in the city's government and economic activities and until his death in 1564 was in effect Geneva's stern spiritual and temporal ruler.

Calvin's pulpit is at the left side of the nave, near the transept. The galleries running along the nave, the transept, and the choir were built to accommodate the overflow

of people listening to the Reformer's sermons. Under Calvin, church attendance was compulsory for all Genevans.

The large organ in the rear of the Cathedral is modern,
installed in 1965. Hour-long performances of compositions
for organ take place on some evenings (watch for announcements in the local newspapers).

The entrance for the ascent of the north tower is in the
left transept. The top terrace offers a panorama of the city,
the lake, the Jura hills, and the Alps. It is open 9 to 11:30
A.M. and 2 to 4:30 P.M. Monday to Saturday. Admission
is $1.90 for adults, 75¢ for children.

The stained-glass windows in the choir are copies of
fifteenth-century works; the originals may be seen in the
Museum of Art and History (p. 186).

The so-called Chapel of the Maccabees, accessible
through a small door at the right side of the nave near the
main entrance, impresses by its late-Gothic flamboyance
and its stained-glass windows. It was built at the beginning
of the fifteenth century and thoroughly restored in the
nineteenth century; Geneva weddings are often solemnized
here.

The small building at the right of the Cathedral, with
steps leading up to a Gothic portal, is the **Auditoire,** or
lecture hall. John Knox and other Reformers preached in
it after Calvin had assigned the structure to a group of
English and Scottish Protestants who had found a refuge
in Geneva.

Turn around for a stroll along the narrow **Rue Jean-
Calvin,** parallel to the Grand-Rue. The Reformer and his
family lived in a plain building at the site of today's No. 11,
an eighteenth-century town house with a commemorative
plaque.

The visitor who instead walks from the outside of the

Cathedral's choir through a vaulted passageway reaches an irregular-shaped square with an eighteenth-century fountain, **Place du Bourg-de-Four.** Remains of ancient Roman ramparts can be seen deep down from the courtyard of the nearby building at 11 Rue de l'Hôtel-de-Ville. The cafés and taverns around the square and in nearby streets are favorites of Geneva students.

At the northeast side of the Place du Bourg-de-Four is a building complex from the early eighteenth century, originally a hospital, which now houses the law courts as **Palace of Justice.** Behind the tribunals, at 2–4 Rue Théodore-de-Bèze, is the **Collège Calvin,** a Renaissance structure with dormers projecting from its high roofs and an attractive outside staircase in the courtyard. Erected in 1558–62, the building was a school and an academy for advanced learning that the Reformer had founded; repaired and enlarged in the nineteenth century and again during the 1980s, it is now a high school. The academy evolved into Geneva University (p. 178).

Nearby is the airy **museum district** with the huge Museum of Art and History (p. 186), other collections, and glimpses of the multidomed Russian Orthodox Church (p. 205). The Rue de la Fontaine leads northward from the Place du Bourg-de-Four to the highest point of the Old Town ramparts, overlooking the modern sections along the southern lakeshore.

To round out the stroll, return to City Hall and go through a neoclassical, columned doorway on the Rue Henry-Fazy to reach the **northwestern ramparts.** The sixteenth-century walls support a spacious promenade with chestnut trees, a stone bench running for 350 feet (108 meters), and a fine view of the gardens and the complex of Geneva University below. The promenade is known as La Treille (The Wine Arbor) because the slope was covered with vineyards before it was incorporated into the fortifications.

The steep **Rampe de la Treille** descends to the **Place Neuve** with the Grand Théâtre (p. 194) and Rath Museum (p. 190). Turn left to the Promenade des Bastions to see the giant **Reformation Monument,** one of Geneva's major landmarks.

Planned and financed by an international committee and designed by a group of French-Swiss architects and sculptors, the huge memorial was started on the four hundredth anniversary of Calvin's birth in 1909 and completed in 1917 during World War I. The monument, rising at the foot of the ramparts, is 328 feet (100 meters) long and 32.8 feet (10 meters) high. It is meant to extol the advance of the entire Reformation movement, not just the achievements of Calvin and his associates, whose statues dominate it. Engraved in the wall of granite and quartz is the Latin motto *Post Tenebras Lux* (After Darkness, Light). At the center four statues, nearly 20 feet (6 meters) high, represent the towering figures of the Reformation in Geneva: Guillaume Farel, who first preached against Roman Catholicism in the city; Calvin; Théodore de Bèze, Calvin's successor in Geneva; and John Knox, founder of the Church of Scotland.

The main group of statues is flanked by six smaller sculptures representing personages who promoted the Reformation in their countries: (from left to right) Fredrick Wilhelm, the Great Elector of Brandenburg (1620–88); William the Silent (1533–84), the leader in the Dutch struggle for independence from Spain; Gaspard de Coligny (1519–72), the French admiral who was the first victim in the Bartholomew's Day massacre of Huguenots; Roger Williams (1603?–83), the advocate of religious freedom in New England and founder of Providence, Rhode Island;

Oliver Cromwell (1599–1658), lord protector of England; and István Bocskay (1557–1606), prince of Transylvania.

Martin Luther and Huldrych Zwingli (p. 57) are not represented by statues, but their names are engraved on the monument. Relief panels between the statues depict various episodes of the Reformation. The bas-relief between the statues of Roger Williams and Cromwell show Pilgrims aboard the *Mayflower* in 1620.

Turning around at the Reformation Monument, the visitor sees, across the park of the Promenade des Bastions, the rear side of **Geneva University,** which had its origin in Calvin's academy, and the vast University Library. The university building was completed in 1872; its main entrance is at 2–4 Rue Candolle (7057111). Several university departments and institutes are scattered throughout the city.

Geneva's Left Bank

Start from the **Pont du Mont-Blanc,** the much-traveled bridge linking the city's two halves at the spot where the Rhône hurtles out of the lake. If you look southward to the foothills of the Mont-Blanc, you see on your right what looks like the sharp prow of a stone ship anchored in the middle of the river. It is an artificial island, built in 1583 to defend the harbor of Geneva from attacks that might come from the lake. The dukes of Savoy who kept coveting the city and its river port in fact maintained a flotilla of armed boats.

The island that was once a bastion of Geneva's fortifications was in 1834 officially dedicated to the memory of Rousseau. As **Ile Rousseau** (Rousseau Island), it is today a public park with tall poplar trees flanking a bronze statue of the writer-philosopher; it can be reached by a footbridge from the Pont des Bergues, which spans the river diagonally behind the Pont du Mont-Blanc.

The southern (left-bank) bridgehead of the Pont du Mont-Blanc is a traffic circle with an underpass for pedestrians. To the left side (for someone coming from the opposite bank) is the **National Monument,** commemorating Geneva's admittance to the Swiss Confederation in 1815. The sculptural group, erected in 1869, represents Helvetia (Switzerland) as a matron being embraced by a delicate-looking younger woman, Geneva.

Nearby is a **flower clock,** its dial 13 feet (four meters) in diameter, of the kind that is seen in many resorts; photos of it grace innumerable picture postcards mailed from Geneva.

The wooded park adjacent to the National Monument is known as the **English Garden** (Jardin Anglais); there are a bandstand and a fountain. Follow the lakefront promenade, Quai Gustave-Ador, to a marina and a pier jutting out into the lake with, offshore, a high plume of water. It is the **Jet d'Eau** (fountain), Geneva's logo-landmark.

A stylized Jet d'Eau has long been the official symbol of the city. Water has been spurting skyward from the surface of the lake since 1886—higher and higher over the years as the pump mechanism was successively strengthened. At present the Jet d'Eau on calm days achieves a height of 475 feet (145 meters). It could reach the top of a thirty-five-story skyscraper and is said to be the world's tallest fountain.

Powerful pumps squirt 135 gallons (500 liters) of lake water into the air every second. The rising, suspended, and falling water and spray form a feather whose shape depends on winds, and which to some extent can be controlled by a throttle from the shore. The Jet d'Eau, floodlit after dark, plays every day until late at night from March to October, and is turned on during cold months for special occasions.

Proceeding along the lakeshore beyond the Jet d'Eau, the stroller sees a larger-than-life statue of an athletic young woman facing the lake, her hair swept back. The modern sculpture is *La Bise*, embodying Geneva's cold, energizing north wind. The lakefront promenade leads to two contiguous municipal gardens, the **Parc de la Grange,** with magnificent roseries, and the **Parc des Eaux-Vives.**

Parallel to the southern lakeshore runs the **Rue du Rhône,** the city's principal shopping street. Behind it are a few quaint squares and lanes as well as ramps ascending to the Old Town.

Right Bank and International District

The **Quai du Mont-Blanc** along the northern lakeshore is Geneva's most elegant promenade. Only on fifty or sixty days every year, when the sky is clear enough, can the white fastnesses of the Mont Blanc massif, 47 miles (75 kilometers) to the southeast, actually be seen from the lakefront. (The peak of Mont-Blanc is 15,772 feet or 4,807 meters in altitude.) Almost always visible, except for dense fog, are the foothills which, like Mont Blanc, are in France: Mont-Salève (p. 208), its cliffs and wooded terraces rising to a ridge with its highest point at 4,287 feet (1,307 meters) south of the city; and the pyramid-shaped Le Môle, which is 3,650 feet (1,113 meters) high, to the southeast.

The big lake boats sail from the docks along Quai du Mont-Blanc. Smartly dressed roller skaters show off their skills on the lakefront, and a miniature railway without rails ferries children and adults along the promenade. Hotels, cafés, and shops catering to tourists face the tree-lined boulevard, a strip on which luxury cars cruise. A bandstand halfway on the Quai du Mont-Blanc is for occasional open-air concerts in summer.

A plaque on the shore parapet near where the Rue des Alpes meets the Quai du Mont-Blanc indicates the point near which Empress Elisabeth of Austria-Hungary, the Bavarian-born "Sissi," was stabbed on September 10, 1898. The restless sixty-one-year-old wife of Emperor Franz Joseph was about to embark for Montreux, accompanied only by a lady-in-waiting, when the twenty-four-year-old Italian anarchist Luigi Luccheni assailed her with a sharp file. She died soon afterward in her suite in the nearby Beau-Rivage Hotel (p. 156).

Diagonally across the boulevard is the **Brunswick Monument,** an extravagant memorial to Duke Karl II of Brunswick (1804–73) in a small park, the Jardin Brunswick. Karl, after having been deposed from his German dukedom during a revolutionary upheaval in 1830, amassed an enormous fortune through successful financial transactions. He bequeathed his riches to the city of Geneva on condition that it should erect for him a monument modeled after the Tombs of the Scaligeri in Verona (the elaborate resting place of the northern Italian city's late-medieval rulers). Geneva faithfully complied with the late duke's will. An equestrian statue of him that originally was to top the Brunswick Monument stands now in the triangular park. The memorial, in Gothic style, includes panels picturing episodes of Brunswick history.

A few hundred yards from the Noga Hilton with its Grand Casino (p. 157) the lakeshore boulevard turns northward and becomes **Quai Wilson.** A breakwater reaching out into the lake was built with stones from Geneva's old fortifications. At the end of that jetty is a lighthouse.

Behind the concrete-and-glass Hôtel Le Président, a

five-star establishment (47 Quai Wilson, phone 7311000, fax 7312206), is a Victorian edifice, the **Palais Wilson.** Once a top-class hotel, it was requisitioned in 1920 to house the League of Nations. A wall plaque acknowledges that President Woodrow Wilson, by promoting the idea of an international organization for the peaceful settlement of conflicts and for cooperation among the countries of the globe, was the real founder of the league. The building served as headquarters of the world body's secretariat from 1920 to 1936, when the league took over its next palatial home (the Palais des Nations; see below). Wilson is credited with having insisted on Geneva as the league's seat.

The Quai Wilson turns into Avenue de France and subsequently Rue de Lausanne, both streets skirting lakeside gardens and mansions with such names as Mon Repos and Perle du Lac. In the latter estate, with entrance at 128 Rue de Lausanne, stands the **Villa Bartholoni,** which was built in 1828 in Italian style for a rich banker. There is also a luxury restaurant, **La Perle du Lac** (7317935).

A modern office building at 154 Rue de Lausanne houses two United Nations agencies, the **General Agreement on Tariff and Trade,** usually referred to by its acronym GATT (7395111); and the **United Nations High Commission for Refugees** (7398111).

Turn left to the broad, rising Avenue de la Paix, which passes the Botanical Garden (p. 192) and at the vast, open Place des Nations reaches the staff entrance to **United Nations headquarters,** with the **Palais des Nations.** (By public transport the Palais des Nations is ten to fifteen minutes from the city center. Take the No. 8 or F bus from the Cornavin rail terminal.)

The European center of the world organization is the Continent's second-biggest edifice next to the Palace of Versailles. A group of five European architects designed in the 1920s what was intended to become a monumental home for the League of Nations. The building complex went up in 1929–36.

The Palais des Nations is a beige stone structure, in most of its parts six stories high, in a style blending neoclassical elements—ornamental half-pillars, an occasional arch—with sober modern lines. The roofs are flat. The main facade, a quarter of a mile (400 meters) long, forms an open court flanked by two side wings and which looks out on the lake across the sloping Ariana Park. These gardens, with century-old trees, now a part of the United Nations enclave, are city property, leased to the world organization. The terrain was once owned and developed by a wealthy Geneva philanthropist and collector, Gustave Revilliod, who named it after his mother, Ariane, and bequeathed it to the city of Geneva. He died in 1890 and is buried in the park.

The League of Nations disbanded in 1946, and its Geneva establishment passed to the newly founded United Nations. The Palais des Nations was enlarged in 1950–52, and a new steel-and-glass E Wing (the *E* stands for east), 262 feet (80 meters) long and looking like a modern hotel, was added in 1973.

The Palais des Nations contains the **Rockefeller Library** in its northern wing. The largest of several gifts to the League of Nations from governments and private donors, the library now comprises about one million volumes and thousands of periodicals; it is also the repository of the defunct league's archives and includes a small United Nations Museum. The reading rooms of the Rockefeller Library are open 8:30 A.M. to 5:30 P.M. Monday to Friday. The Entrance is at 8–14 Avenue de la Paix (7310211).

The E Wing houses a **Philatelic Museum;** on view are mail stamps issued by the world organization and by governments around the globe. The museum is open 9 to 11 A.M. and 2 to 4 P.M. Monday to Friday.

Hour-long guided tours of the Palais des Nations are conducted, with commentaries in English and other languages, 9 A.M. to noon and 2 to 5 P.M. Monday to Friday. Admission is $3.75 for adults, $1.50 for children. For information and reservations, call 7346011, extension 4539. The entrance is at 8–14 Avenue de la Paix. Visitors are shown marble galleries, the large General Assembly Hall and other meeting rooms, and some of the many works of art and other gifts to the old league and to the United Nations.

Admission to the Ariana Park is free during United Nations office hours. The gardens, too, contain sculptures and other objects from various parts of the world. The United Nations complex, including the leased terrain, is legally under the jurisdiction of the world organization and is policed by its own security personnel in uniform and in plain clothes.

On the grounds of the Ariana Park, facing the west facade of the United Nations Palace, is the **Ariana Museum** (p. 190), a domed building in revival Renaissance style that Revilliod commissioned in the late 1870s as a home for his collections. The museum has lately been closed for restoration.

Leaving the United Nations Palace through the visitors' entrance, one sees on a hill across the Avenue de la Paix, at No. 17, the **headquarters of the International Committee of the Red Cross** (7346001). The building was once a hotel. The Red Cross was established by the Geneva Convention of 1864, largely owing to the lobbying efforts by the Geneva-born banker and humanitarian Jean-Henri Dunant.

Adjacent to the headquarters building is the **Interna-**

tional Museum of the Red Cross and Red Crescent (p. 191). Nancy Reagan, wife of the U.S. president, and Raisa Gorbacheva, wife of the secretary general of the Soviet Communist party, were on hand in 1985 when the cornerstone of the structure was laid. The museum was opened in 1989, 125 years after the founding of the Red Cross.

Nearby are the central offices of several other international bodies. Among them are the following:

International Labor Organization (ILO), 4 Route Morillon (7996111), a specialized agency of the United Nations, is housed in a modern building completed in 1973.

World Health Organization (WHO), 20 Avenue Appia (7912111), has interesting art in the lobby of its building (built in 1966) and in its own park.

World Meteorological Organization, 41 Avenue Giuseppe-Motta (7308111).

International Telecommunications Union (ITU), Place des Nations (7305111).

World Council of Churches, 150 Route de Ferney (7916111), is an interfaith body in which most Christian denominations are represented. The Roman Catholic Church is not a full member.

The **International Conference Center,** 3 Rue Varembé (7919111), opened in 1973, has a large auditorium with seats for 800 delegates and, in the galleries, for 150 spectators beside smaller halls and meeting rooms, all with facilities for simultaneous translations and audio-video broadcasting. Designed for international governmental meetings, the center is also available for private conventions.

The headquarters of the **European Center for Nuclear Research (CERN)** is in the suburb of Meyrin (7676111), about 3.5 miles (6 kilometers) west of central Geneva, near the French border (No. 15 bus to the CERN stop). The installations of this huge research laboratory are mostly underground in an area four-fifths of which are in neighboring France. They include two particle accelerators, one 17 miles (27 kilometers), the other 4.4 miles (7 kilometers) in circumference. The research center, financed by fourteen European governments, employs a permanent staff of 3,500 and is visited by hundreds of scientists each year.

Museums and Collections

Most of Geneva's museums are closed on Monday. Admission to several public collections was still free in 1993, but for budgetary reasons the city was contemplating charging entrance fees.

Museum of Art and History, 2 Rue Charles-Galland (3290011), is a five-minute stroll southeast of the Cathedral (No. 6 bus from the Cornavin rail terminal). Open 10 A.M. to 5 P.M. Tuesday to Sunday. The large building in eclectic beaux arts style, which opened in 1910, is the principal landmark of Geneva's so-called museum district. It contains half a million exhibits tracing humankind's and Geneva's development from prehistory to the present. Opposite the main entrance is a larger-than-life sculpture from the museum's collections, Henry Moore's *Reclining Figure with Arched Leg.*

From the lobby, stairways lead to the various exhibition levels. Most visitors first ascend to the second floor (fourth level), containing paintings and sculptures from the Middle Ages to the twentieth century.

The museum's and Geneva's pride is the famous altarpiece, *The Miraculous Draught of Fishes*, by Konrad Witz, painted in 1444 for the city's Cathedral (Room 401). The artist represents the Sea of Galilee, where Jesus performs the miracle (Luke 5:1–7), as the Lake of Geneva seen from the north shore. The harbor, the fortifications and fields, and the mountainscape in the background are realistically rendered.

The picture gallery also boasts works by masters of the Flemish and Dutch schools of the sixteenth and seventeenth centuries, and by Swiss, French, and Italian painters of these and more recent periods. Ferdinand Hodler, who started his artistic career in Geneva and lived in the city until his death in 1918, is represented with many paintings and studies. There are also a few works by Cézanne, Corot, Monet, Picasso, and Renoir, as well as sculptures by Rodin and Alberto Giacometti.

The lower levels of the museum contain prehistoric finds; a stupendous archeological collection with well-labeled Egyptian, near-Eastern, Greek, pre-Roman, and Roman antiquities; a medieval section; and a collection of weapons, furniture, and art objects.

Natural History Museum, 1 Route de Malagnou (7359130), east of the Museum of Art and History, is one of the Continent's largest institutions of its kind. Open 10 A.M. to 5 P.M. Tuesday to Sunday. The collections, assembled since the end of the eighteenth century and enlarged by prominent scientists, were reorganized in the vast modern building, opened in 1966. Walking the entire circuit of more than a mile (nearly 2 kilometers) on three levels, the visitor sees dinosaurs, dioramas of Alpine and exotic fauna, minerals, and a wealth of other items.

Ethnographical Museum, 65–67 Boulevard Carl-Vogt (3281218), is west of the university. Open 10 A.M. to noon and 2 to 5 P.M. Tuesday to Sunday. An annex of the museum is in the suburb of Conches, 7 Chemin Calandrini (3460125), 3 miles (nearly 5 kilometers) southeast of the city center, open 10 A.M. to 5 P.M. Wednesday to Sunday. The vast collection comprises thousands of items related to popular culture, art, and handicrafts of the Rhône Valley as well as from elsewhere in Europe and other continents. The Conches annex is used mainly for temporary exhibitions.

Modern Art Museum (Petit Palais), 2 Terrasse Saint-Victor (3461433), is south of the Museum of Art and History. Open 10 A.M. to noon and 2 to 6 P.M. Tuesday to Sunday, 2 to 6 P.M. Monday. Admission: $3.50, students $2.50. The "Little Palace" is an elegant townhouse of the 1860s, now the showcase of French modern works assembled by Oscar Ghez, a Tunisian resident of Geneva. The private collection ranges from impressionist to mid-twentieth-century art and includes paintings by many lesser-known French painters of the impressionist, postimpressionist, and naïf currents. The Petit Palais also serves as the setting for periodic special shows and seminars.

Maison Tavel, 6 Rue du Puits-Saint-Pierre (3102900), is near the Arsenal. Open 10 A.M. to 5 P.M. Tuesday to Sunday. The Tavel House is a restored medieval dwelling in which a succession of wealthy families lived; it is believed to be Geneva's oldest surviving residential building. It contains period furniture, a completely equipped ancient kitchen, elaborate business signs, and early-nineteenth-century paintings of lake scenes in which amateur fishermen are shown wearing high hats in their rowboats. There are also underground storerooms, a deep cistern, and an attic hall with an 1850 scale model of Geneva, house by house. The ruin of a Romanesque tower in the courtyard has become a wishing well into which visitors fling small coins.

Watchmaking and Enamel Work Museum, 15 Route de Malagnou (7367412), is near the Natural History Museum. Open 10 A.M. to 5 P.M. Wednesday to Monday.

This collection, dedicated to a Genevan skill and industry, occupies a graceful eighteenth-century villa in a garden. It displays timepieces of all periods and is being continually enriched with novelties. One room contains the reconstruction of a Geneva watchmaker's workshop. The exhibits aren't limited to the products of Swiss craftsmen; there are also historic German, French, English, and Italian clocks and watches. A local minor art, painting on enamel, is illustrated by many fine examples.

Baur Collection, 8 Rue Munier-Romilly (3461729), is south of the Museum of Art and History. Open 2 to 6 P.M. Tuesday to Sunday. Admission: $2.25. This is one of Europe's largest hoards of Chinese and Japanese art, gathered by the Swiss businessman Albert Baur, who in his younger years was based in what was then Ceylon (now Sri Lanka), and who until his death in 1951 kept purchasing new pieces. Many of the collection's seven thousand objects are on permanent display; others are shown periodically.

Museum of Old Musical Instruments, 23 Rue François-Le-Fort (3469565), is east of the Museum of Art and History. Open 3 to 6 P.M. Tuesday, 10 A.M. to noon and 3 to

6 P.M. Thursday, 8 to 10 P.M. Friday, or by telephone appointment (3114388). Admission: 75¢. Now owned by the city, this collection of nearly four hundred ancient musical instruments was created by two musicians, Fritz Ernst and Elise-Isolde Clerc. The exhibits include rare pieces from the sixteenth and seventeenth centuries. Some of the instruments are occasionally played during concerts of ancient music in the second-floor hall.

Ariana Museum, 10 Avenue de la Paix (7342950), near the United Nations complex, one of Europe's most important ceramics collections, was in 1993 still closed for reorganization.

Jean-Jacques Rousseau Museum, Public and University Library, Promenade des Bastions (3208266), adjoins the university. Open 9 A.M. to noon and 2 to 5 P.M. Monday to Friday, 9 A.M. to noon Saturday. Free admission. A collection of documents and other memorabilia connected with the life and works of Geneva's famous native son.

Voltaire Museum, 25 Rue des Délices (3447133), is near the right bank of the Rhône. Open 2 to 5 P.M. Monday to Friday. Free admission. The museum shares an early-eighteenth-century building in a small park with the Voltaire Institute, essentially a research library with twenty thousand volumes. The French writer-philosopher lived here in 1755–60. Four showrooms contain portraits of Voltaire, manuscripts, documents, early editions of his works, and furniture owned and used by him. There is also a life-size statue of Voltaire, clad in a period costume, seated in front of his desk; the writer Pierre-Augustin Caron de Beaumarchais, the author of *The Marriage of Figaro*, commissioned the sculpture of his idol in 1781.

Rath Museum, Place Neuve (3214388), is located at the

right side of the Grand Théâtre. Open 10 A.M. to noon and
2 to 6 P.M. Tuesday to Sunday, also 8 to 10 P.M. Wednesday
(subject to change). Admission fees vary. Now used for
temporary art shows and special exhibitions, this was Geneva's principal art museum until 1910. It was built in the
Greek style with a columned portico in 1825 as a memorial
to Simon Rath, who as a general in the Imperial Russian
army had acquired substantial wealth and an art collection,
and who died in retirement in Geneva in 1819.

Barbier-Müller Museum, 10 Rue Jean-Calvin (3120270),
is in the Old Town. Open 11 A.M. to 5 P.M. daily. Admission: $3.50, students $2.20. This is a private collection of
primitive art, mainly from Africa, Indonesia, and Oceania,
with some pieces from the Western Hemisphere. Noteworthy are a mask from the Congo, which belonged to
the French painter André Derain, and a golden mask from
Peru.

Zoubov Foundation, 2 Rue des Granges (7327954), is in
the Old Town. Guided tours at 6 P.M. Thursday and 2:30
P.M. Saturday from October 1 to June 14; special visits can
be arranged on request. Admission: $2.25. Donated to the
city by the Zoubov family as a memorial for a daughter
who died in a car accident at the age of eighteen, the collection, left by Countess Tatiana Zoubov, consists of
eighteenth-century furniture, old paintings, and art objects
from Europe and China.

**International Museum of the Red Cross and Red Cres-
cent,** 17 Avenue de la Paix (7345248), is adjacent to the
headquarters of the International Committee of the Red
Cross. Open 10 A.M. to 5 P.M. Wednesday to Monday.
Admission: $7. The steel-and-glass structure contains sev-
eral display areas with documents, photos, and other mate-

rial relating to humanitarian work in various parts of the world in the recent and more remote past. There are also audiovisual presentations of current projects, films, and a special show on human rights.

Random Sights and Strolls

The **Botanical Garden,** adjacent to the Ariana Park and United Nations headquarters, is accessible through an underpass from the Rue de Lausanne beyond GATT headquarters. It is open 7 A.M. to 6:30 P.M., in winter 8 A.M. to 5 P.M. Admission is free. The administrative building of the Botanical Garden is at 1 Jardin de l'Impératrice (7326969). Lush vegetation, flower beds, little ponds, winding paths, a rock garden with Alpine flora, plenty of twittering birds, a deer park, and tropical plants in greenhouses make this a restful place. There is a terrace with cafeteria service. Across the Rue de Lausanne, close to the lake, is the Botanical Conservatory, in a ninety-year-old building with statues of outstanding botanists. It contains a rich collection of dried plants and a botanical library. Scientists and students may ask for admission (7326969).

Carouge is an old neighborhood on the city's southern outskirts with a distinctive Italianate flavor—a Little Piedmont. Take the No. 12 trolleycar from Rue du Rhône or Place Neuve on the left bank of the Rhône, and get off about ten minutes later at the second stop (Marché) after crossing the little Arve River, a tributary of the Rhône. You will find yourself in a piazza that might be the center of some small town near Turin with market stands, a fountain, and low eighteenth-century houses. The village of Carouge, until 1815 a part of the Kingdom of Sardinia-Piedmont, was once a smugglers' lair and a haven for

Genevans who were fed up with their city's puritanism. The entire district has been officially declared to be "of national importance," tantamount to a historic-landmark designation. Lately Swiss and foreign artists have moved into the area, followed by the start of gentrification with new boutiques and bohemian cafés.

Stroll around the streets of Carouge, which are laid out in a grid pattern. Look at the plane trees, the dignified old buildings with elaborate doorways, and the Holy Cross Church, a baroque edifice between the Place du Marché and the Place de Sardaigne (Sardinia Square).

Periodic art exhibitions are held at the Carouge Museum, 2 Place de Sardaigne (3423383).

BEYOND SIGHTSEEING

Music in Geneva

The foremost classical-music body of French-speaking Switzerland, the **Orchestre de la Suisse Romande,** is based in Geneva. The administrative offices are at 3 Promenade du Pin (3292511), behind the Museum of Art and History. The Society of the Friends of the Orchestre de la Suisse Romande, whose members enjoy priority for concert tickets and season subscriptions, has its headquarters at 3A Rue Moillebeau (7330040), near the district of international organizations.

The Orchestre de la Suisse Romande was founded by the conductor Ernest Ansermet (1883–1969) at the end of World War I. Lovers of classical music everywhere know his name from the many recordings, especially of modern compositions, that he produced with his orchestra. Today the orchestra is a foundation administered by representatives of the State of Geneva and other French-speaking cantons as well as private cultural organizations.

The orchestra gives regular symphonic concerts in the one-hundred-year-old Victoria Hall, Rue Joseph-Hornung and Rue Général-Dufour near the Place Neuve. Watch the local newspapers and wall posters for program information, or call 7330040. The box office of the Victoria Hall (3288121) is staffed only on evenings when concerts or recitals are scheduled. Ticket prices are $7.50 to $50; for some subscription concerts the odd unclaimed ticket might be available.

Opera is performed in the **Grand Théâtre,** Place Neuve (3112318; box office, 3112311). The Grand Théâtre, erected in 1879, looks like a scale model of the opera house in Paris that Charles Garnier built a few years earlier. The Geneva theater was designed by the architect J. Elysée Goss and financed with part of the legacy bequeathed to the city by the duke of Brunswick. The Grand Théâtre opened with Rossini's *Guglielmo Tell*, the work celebrating the Swiss national hero William Tell. After a fire in 1951 the theater was restructured; it now has some fifteen hundred seats.

Subsidized by the city and the Canton of Geneva, the Grand Théâtre produces operas and ballets during its season from September to the end of June. Members of the Orchestre de la Suisse Romande provide the music, and international singers are often signed up. The theater has its own chorus and ballet troupe. World-class stars are occasionally heard in Grand Théâtre recitals.

While it may be difficult to obtain a seat for a subscription performance, ticket sales are unrestricted for some operatic evenings and for most recitals. Ticket prices range from $15 for the cheapest seat at a repertoire performance to $87 for an orchestra seat at a gala.

Visiting orchestras and soloists occasionally perform in the Victoria Hall (discussed earlier in this section). Chamber music and soloists can often be heard at the **Music Conservatory,** built in 1868, on Place Neuve (3117633), left of the Grand Théâtre.

Pop music, jazz, and rock are frequently performed at the **Grand Casino,** 19 Quai du Mont-Blanc (7319811) in the Noga Hilton complex (p. 157). Visiting dance troupes may also be seen there.

Theater

Classic French drama and modern plays are staged at *La Comédie*, 6 Boulevard des Philosophes (3205001), south of the university; and in the *Théâtre de Carouge*, 39 Rue Ancienne (3434343), in the Carouge district. Modern French-language productions can also be seen at the *Théâtre de Saint-Gervais*, 5 Rue du Temple (7322060), on the right bank of the Rhône; and *Nouveau Théâtre de Poche*, 7 Rue du Cheval-Blanc (3103759), on the southern outskirts. Revues, sketches, and variety shows are occasionally offered at the Grand Casino (see preceding section). Puppet shows are put on at *Théâtre des Marionettes de Genève*, 3 Rue Rodo (3296767), on the right (north) bank of the Arve River.

Cinema

Major movie houses are **ABC,** 42 Rue du Rhône (3102018), on the main shopping street; **Central,** 23 Rue Chantepoulet (7324514); **Le Plaza,** 1–3 Rue Chantepoulet (7325700); and **Rialto,** Place Cornavin (7327050)—all three near the

Cornavin rail terminal—and **Les Rex,** 8 Rue de la Confédération (3296648), in the Confédération Centre mall.

CAC-Voltaire, 27 Rue Voltaire (3449444), on the right bank of the Rhône, screens revivals, often in the original language. Consult local newspapers on programs, starting times, and to find out whether films are shown with their original soundtrack (*version originale* or *v.o.*) or with subtitles (*s.tit.*).

Night Life

Activities in Geneva's night spots may become hectic during diplomatic conferences and the periodic international trade shows and conventions. The large number of resident foreigners, many of them single and quite a few well paid, keeps the two dozen or so reputable and semireputable discotheques and nightclubs in business, although native Genevans tend to go to bed early, and the streets of the city center and the suburbs are deserted after 9 P.M. Some night spots open every evening and close at 3 A.M., others concentrate on the weekend business. Prices are generally stiff.

Geneva's largest discotheque is **Arthur's,** 20 Route de Pré-Bois (7881600), underneath the modern, five-star Mövenpick-Radisson Hotel (7987575). Among the several other night spots, **Club 58,** 15 Rue des Glacis-de-Rive (7351515), is a discotheque and cabaret near the central Rue du Rhône. Also: **Blue Chip** and **Club 19,** 19 Quai du Mont-Blanc (7319811 and 7315735), both in the Noga Hilton (p. 157); and **Moulin Rouge,** 1 Avenue du Mail (3293566), west of the Place Neuve.

Harry's New-York Bar, 8 Rue de la Confédération (3294421), on the street floor of the Confédération Centre mall, is a much-frequented piano bar. Dinner music in the

Swiss folklore mode, with alphorn and yodelers, can be heard at **Restaurant Edelweiss,** 2 Place de la Navigation (7314940); and gypsy music accompanies dinner at **Impératrice Sissi,** 32 Rue de Lausanne (7325292). The two latter restaurants are in the Les Pâquis section between the northern lakefront and the railroad tracks, an area honeycombed with cafés and night spots.

Gambling starts at noon daily in the Salle des Jeux (Gaming Hall) of the Grand Casino, 19 Quai du Mont-Blanc (7326320), in the Noga Hilton complex. Only a comparatively bland game of chance—boule—and slot machines are legal forms of casino gambling in Geneva. High-stakes players cross the lake by boat or go by car to Évian-les-Bains, the French spa on the lake's southern shore, 25 miles (40 kilometers) from Geneva, where the roulette wheels spin at the local casino.

Folklore

Once a year the sober Genevans indulge in revelry. The occasion is each anniversary of **L'Escalade,** or Scaling of the Walls, on the night of December 11–12, 1602, when the citizenry repelled an attempted invasion. The attackers were the troops of Duke Charles Emmanuel I of Savoy, who had deemed the time ripe for realizing his old dream of reasserting his dynasty's claim to control of Geneva.

To the Genevans, the duke was "The Cat." Using collapsible ladders, handpicked Savoyard soldiers climbed over the walls into the city from the west side at a spot now marked by a plaque in the Rue de la Corraterie. They were massacred by the inhabitants. The most famous episode of the nocturnal battle was the feat of Mère Royaume, wife of the director of Geneva's mint, who from a window threw a tureen with boiling soup on the invaders. (Sculp-

tures on No. 5 and No. 7 Rue de la Corraterie commemo-
rate Mère Royaume's deed.) The forces of the duke of
Savoy retreated, and the Genevans hanged thirteen Savoyard prisoners.

Hot soup, recalling Mère Royaume's cauldron, is ladled
out to merrymakers up and down the Old Town during
the Escalade celebrations, which are held on the weekend
before December 11. In homes all over Geneva candy-
filled chocolate replicas of Mère Royaume's tureen, the
marmite, delight children, and they don costumes to roam
bistros and cafés, trick-or-treat style.

The children chant "Cé qu'è laîno," a popular song
on the Escalade events in the local dialect of the early
seventeenth century, which sounds archaic today. It has no
fewer than sixty-eight stanzas, the first of which, in English
translation, goes like this:

> *The Lord on high, the Lord of hosts*
> *All scoundrels does He mock, deride*
> *He truly showed that Saturday night*
> *That He was on Geneva's side.*

A masked ball is held on the eve of the Escalade festivities. The day afterward an alarm is sounded at the Cathedral, and Genevan men in armor, carrying pikes and
blunderbusses, ride horses through the narrow streets and
squares of the Old Town. On the last day a torchlight
procession shuffles up the Grand-Rue to a bonfire in front
of the Cathedral.

Unconnected with the Escalade commemoration, several scores—often hundreds—of hardened Genevans, men
and women, jump into the icy Rhône on the morning of
the middle Sunday in December to compete in a 142-yard

(130-meter) swimming race between two bridges. The contest, held every year since 1949, is known as the Coupe de Noël (Christmas Cup). It always attracts hundreds of onlookers wrapped in furs and warm coats.

Exercise

Jogging. The promenades on the lake's north and south shores as well as the city's vast parks are the most suitable areas.

Swimming. Genève-Plage, Port Noir, Quai Gustave-Ador (7362482), on the lake's south shore beyond the Parc des Eaux-Vives, reachable by No. 2 bus, is a large bathing concession with a restaurant (7362240). Admission is $3 for all but children under twelve, who pay $1.50. Closer to the city center, and often crowded, is Pâquis-Plage at the end of Quai du Mont-Blanc (7322974), on the break-water that juts out from the north shore into an area in the lake where currents suck water into the Rhône. This facility is open all year. Also on the north shore, close to the United Nations complex and patronized by many staff members of international organizations: Plage Le Repo-soir, 222 Rue de Lausanne (7324265); and Plage ONU, Le Port, Route de Lausanne (7316829). For public swimming pools, see the Geneva telephone directory under *Piscines*.

Tennis. Only one among Geneva's leading hotels has ten-nis courts, La Réserve (p. 158), far out on the Route de Lausanne. It's not always easy to rent a court in the city because of the great demand. Try Tennis Club Genève in the Parc des Eaux-Vives (7355350); the municipal tennis courts at 29 Route de Vessy (7841420), on the far southern outskirts; or any of the clubs listed in the Geneva telephone directory under *Tennis*.

Bicycling. Rent bicycles at the Cornavin rail terminal. Riding a bike is something of a feat in the dense traffic of Geneva's center, but the lake promenades have cycling lanes.

Golf. Visitors have a hard time playing a round of golf in or near Geneva because the available courses are usually overbooked. The leading local Golf Club de Genève has its links at 70 Route de la Capite (7357540) in the suburb of Cologny on the lake's south shore, but you will need excellent connections to get in. The Swiss Golf Association, 19 Place Croix-Blanche, 1066 Épalinges (021-7843531), near Lausanne, will give advice on where a visitor may play golf within a reasonable distance from Geneva. The chances to get on a fairway are better in nearby France. Try the eighteen-hole course of the Royal Club at Évian-les-Bains (023-50751400).

Horseback riding. Nouveau Manège de Geneve, 233 Route de la Capite (7523844), is in the village of Vesenaz on the southern lakeshore; Manège d'Onex, 5 Chemin Gustave-Rochette (7921688), is in the village of Onex, west of Geneva. Both riding establishments can be reached by car in twenty to thirty minutes from the city center.

Skiing. The favorite ski slopes of the Genevans are in France's nearby Savoy (Savoie) region, where new roads, ski lifts, and other infrastructures were created for the 1992 Winter Olympic Games with the town of Albertville as their center. The winter sports resorts of the Swiss cantons of Vaud and Valais—Villars-sur-Ollon, Crans-Montana, Champéry, Zermatt, and others—are at least two hours by car or railroad from Geneva.

Ice-skating. Patinoire Vernets, 4–6 Rue Hans-Wilsdorf (3438850), in summer an outdoor swimming pool, is on

the left bank of the Arve River on the southwestern outskirts. It has a restaurant, Le Chalet Suisse (3432071).

Spectator Sports

The leading Geneva **professional soccer** team is Football
Club Servette, with its stadium at Chemin des Sports
(3450666), on the western outskirts. Championship games
always attract thousands of home team supporters as well
as fans of the visiting team.

The Bol d'Or (Golden Bowl Trophy) **sailing race** on
the second Sunday after Pentecost in May or June has been
held on the lake since 1930 and is now a classic. Hundreds
of boats enter each event, and many thousands of spectators
line the shores.

Two international **tennis** tournaments are held in Geneva every year: the Challenger of Geneva (men) at the
Drizia-Miremont Club, 6 Route de Vessy (3473824) in
August, and the Barcley Open at the Eaux-Vives courts
(p. 199) in September.

The World Cup International **Horse-Jumping** Com-
petition takes place in the Palexpo (p. 208, 7981111) every
December.

The Christmas Cup **swimming** race (pp. 198–99) has
become a piece of Geneva folklore.

Emergencies

The **police emergency number** is 117. For nonemergency calls, look in the Geneva telephone directory under
Gendarmerie and **Police**.

The **fire department emergency number** is 118.

In case of **medical emergencies**, call 144 for an ambulance, or dial 3202511 for twenty-four-hour medical ser-

vice, or, if you want an urgent house visit by a physician, call 7811777 (service around the clock).

The University and Cantonal Hospital, 24 Rue Micheli-du-Crest (3226111), south of the Old Town, operates a twenty-four-hour emergency ward. For other institutions of Geneva's vast and prestigious medical establishment (some also with twenty-four-hour emergency services), consult the telephone directory under *Cliniques*, *Homes*, and *Hôpitaux*.

Services

Post offices are open 7:30 to 6 P.M. Monday to Friday, and 7:30 to 11 A.M. Saturday (closed Sunday). The main post, telegraph, and telephone office, PTT 1, is at 18 Rue du Mont-Blanc, about halfway between the Cornavin rail terminal and the lakefront. An express counter at PTT 2, 16 Rue des Gares, behind the Cornavin rail terminal, is open 6 A.M. to 10:45 P.M. Monday to Friday, 6 A.M. to 9 P.M. Saturday, and 9 A.M. to 12:30 P.M. and 3 to 10 P.M. Sunday (higher rates are charged). The post office of the United Nations complex is PTT 10, 8 Avenue de la Paix.

Banks are open 8:30 A.M. to 4:30 P.M. Monday to Friday (until 5:30 P.M. on Wednesday). Money exchange offices at the Cornavin rail terminal and at Geneva Airport open at 6 A.M. and close at 9:45 P.M. (rail terminal) and 11 P.M. (airport) daily.

Public offices are generally open from 8:30 or 9 A.M. to 4:30 or 5 P.M. Monday to Friday. For departments and agencies, look in the Geneva telephone directory under *Administration cantonale* and *Administration municipale*.

Additional services are as follows:

Alcoholics Anonymous. The phone number for the En-

glish-speaking Intergroup is 3108115; Spanish, 7327169.
For Al-Anon (English), call 7961979.

Babysitters. Many listings will be found in the Geneva
telephone directory under *Garderies d'enfants*.

Consulates. The United States Consulate, 1–3 Avenue de
la Paix (7387613), is near the United Nations complex.
The British Consulate General, 37–39 Rue Vermont
(7332385), is near the district of international organizations. The address of the Canadian Consulate is 1 Chemin
Pré-de-la-Bichette (7339000); that of the Australian Consulate, 56–58 Rue de Moillebeau (7346200).

Dentists. These are listed in the Geneva telephone directory under *Medecins-dentistes*. For emergencies, the private
dental clinics Malombré, 5 Chemin Malombré (3466444),
in the city's southeast, and Servette, 60 Avenue Wendt
(7339800), in the city's west, are staffed 7:30 A.M. to 8 P.M.
Monday to Saturday, and alternately on Sunday.

Lawyers. See listings under *Avocats* in the Geneva telephone directory.

Libraries. Bibliothèque Publique et Universitaire, Promenade des Bastions (3208266), is open 9 A.M. to noon and
2 to 6 P.M. Monday to Friday, and 9 A.M. to noon Saturday.
 Bibliotheca Bodmeriana, 19–21 Route Guignard
(7362370), in the suburb of Cologny on the lake's south
shore, is one of the world's major private collections of
precious manuscripts and rare books. It is open 2 to 6 P.M.
Thursday, and 6 to 8 P.M. on the first Tuesday of each
month. In June to September it is open 2 to 5 P.M. Saturday. Admission is $1.90; students pay $1.10. The collection, housed in a distinguished mansion, was assembled by
Martin Bodmer, a wealthy scholar who was vice president

of Geneva's Red Cross during World War II. Now owned by the Martin Bodmer Foundation, the library is continually enlarged with support from the Canton of Geneva. Among the collection's many bibliographic treasures are the world's oldest manuscript attributed to St. John the Evangelist, Greek and Coptic papyri, the only Gutenberg Bible in Switzerland, and manuscripts and first editions of works by authors from Goethe and Rousseau to Kafka.

The office that handles **lost property** *(objets trouvés)* is at 7 Glacis-de-Rive (7876111) off Rue du Rhône.

Pharmacies. Thus listed in the Geneva telephone directory, pharmacies are numerous in the city. Some pharmacies stay open on a rotating basis until 9 P.M., some until 11 P.M., and some have all-night service. To find out about late-hour schedules, call 111.

Public toilets. Facilities can be found at the Cornavin rail terminal, in front of the main post office, underground in front of the Cathedral, in the central Place Saint-Gervais on the right bank of the Rhône, and in some other squares.

Religious services. Geneva offers visitors many opportunities for worship.

National Protestant Church of Geneva: Services in French at the Cathedral of St. Peter (3297598) at 10 A.M. Sunday; also at the sixteenth-century Temple of Saint-Gervais, Place du Temple (7326734), on the right bank of the Rhône; at the Temple de la Fusterie, Place de la Fusterie (3115009), on the left bank of the Rhône, near Rue de la Confédération; and at the Temple de Pâquis, 48 Rue de Berne (7311418) in the Pâquis section.

Protestant services in English: American Church (Episcopal), 3 Rue de Monthoux (7328078), in the Pâquis section. Holy Trinity Church (Church of England), Rue du Mont-Blanc (7315155), a Tudor-style edifice (1854) in a little park near the lakefront. Auditorium of Calvin (Church of Scotland), 1 Place de la Taconnerie (7982909), near the Cathedral. Lutheran Church, 20 Rue Verdaine (3104187), in the Old Town. Evangelical Baptist Church, 7 Rue Cherbuliez (7868211), on the eastern outskirts. Church of the Living Savior (Pentecostal), 20 Avenue Ernest-Pictet (3447070), on the southeastern outskirts. Adventist Church, 13 Rue Musy (7351314), in the city's northeast. First Church of Christ, Scientist, 8 Boulevard des Philosophes (3291561), south of the Old Town. Church of Jesus Christ of Latter-Day Saints, 32 Avenue Louis Casaï (7986136), near Cointrin Airport. Church of Christ, 25 Rue de la Terrassière (7355756), near the museum district. International Christian Fellowship of Geneva, 3 Rue Jean-Charles-Amat (7328640), in the Pâquis section.

Protestant services in Spanish: Temple du Plainpalais, 31 Avenue du Mail (7336664), west of the university.

Roman Catholic: Masses in French at the Basilica of Nôtre-Dame, Place Cornavin (7323157), at 7:30, 9, 10, and 11:30 A.M. and 5 and 8:30 P.M. Sunday, 10 and 11:30 A.M. and 6 P.M. Saturday. Masses in English: Basilica of Nôtre-Dame, at 7 P.M. Sunday. Also at John XXIII Center, Geneva's parish church for English-speaking Roman Catholics, 35 Chemin Adolphe-Pasteur (7330483), on the northwestern outskirts. Masses in Spanish: Misión Católica, 18 Rue du Général-Dufour (3108060), near the Place Neuve.

Russian Orthodox: Cathedral of the Holy Cross, 3 Rodolphe-Toepffer (3464709), rises in the museum district. The Byzantine-style church was built in 1865 with

funds provided by the Russian imperial family. Enlarged
in 1916, the edifice is crowned by six gilt domes and in its
interior is adorned with many icons.

Synagogues: The oldest Jewish house of worship in
Geneva (Ashkenazic) is in the Place de la Synagogue
(3204686), west of the Place Neuve. Geneva's Sephardim
worship at Synagogue Hekhal Haness, 54 ter Route de
Malagnou (7369632), on the city's eastern outskirts. Orthodox synagogue: 2 Place des Eaux-Vives (7352298),
near the southern lakefront. Liberal Jewish Community:
12 Quai du Seujet (7323245), on the right bank of the
Rhone. The Jewish Community of Geneva (Communauté
Israélite) has offices at 10 Rue Saint-Léger (3404686), near
the university; rabbinate, 7812126.

Mosque: 34 Chemin Colladon (7983711), near the district of international organizations. Islamic Center: 13 Avenue de Grenade (7865098), in the city's northeast.

Tourist information. Office du Tourisme de Genève,
Service Renseignements, Cornavin rail terminal (7385200,
fax 7319056), is open 9 A.M. to 6 P.M. Monday to Saturday.
The official Tourist Office publishes a weekly bulletin, *La
Semaine à Genève/ This Week in Geneva*, with city news,
listings of special events, schedules of museums and exhibitions, theater programs, and much advertising in French
and English. The bulletin is available free at hotels and at
the Tourist Information Office at the rail terminal.

Travel services. The Geneva telephone directory lists the
city's many travel bureaus under *Agences de voyages*.

Shopping and Trade Shows

Geneva's main shopping area is the left-bank Rue du
Rhône, its side streets, and the nearby Rue de la Confédéra-

tion. Jewelry and watch shops and fashion boutiques are dominant. The glittering Confédération Centre at 8 Rue de la Confédération is a multilevel shopping mall with boutiques, a movie theater, a brasserie, and a piano bar. The building houses the Geneva Stock Exchange (Bourse de Genève, 3100684) as well. Many stores also line the Rue du Mont-Blanc on the right bank, and the lake and river embankments.

The leading **department stores** are Au Grand Passage, 50 Rue du Rhône (3206611) on the left bank, and La Placette, 9 Rue Grenus (7317400), near the Cornavin rail terminal.

Bookstores include the chain Payot & Naville S.A., with branches at 6 Rue Grenus (7318950), near La Placette department store; 5 Rue de la Confédération (3109266); and other locations around town. The United Nations Bookshop is in the United Nations complex, 8–14 Avenue de la Paix (7341473).

Many old-book shops are on the Grand-Rue and other streets and squares in the Old Town and around the university. Look for *Livres anciens* in the listings of *Librairies* in the Geneva telephone directory.

Geneva's **art trade** is thriving. More than 150 commercial art galleries, many of them in the Old Town, offer antiquities, primitive art, old masters, oriental art, modern and contemporary paintings and sculptures, graphics, precious tapestries, and curios. Listings are in the Geneva telephone directory under *Galeries* and *Galeries d'art*.

The city has lately become one of the world's major auction centers especially for gems, jewelry, precious watches, and other small, valuable objects. Major sales are held in May and November when international buyers and collectors flock to Geneva.

Leading international auction houses maintain permanent offices in Geneva: Christie's, 8 Place de la Taconnerie (3102544); Habsburg-Feldman, 202 Route de Grand-Lancy, Onex (7572530); Sotheby's, 13 Quai du Mont-Blanc (7328585); and Phillips Son & Neale, 10 Rue Chaudronnière (3106828).

Geneva's **flea market** is held in the Plaine du Plainpalais, a large square west of the Place Neuve, every Wednesday and Saturday. Habitués browse among old books, old clocks, and bric-a-brac. The **flower market** in the central Place du Molard, off the Rue du Rhône, is held every weekday morning; the clothing and book market in the nearby Place de la Madeleine also takes place daily except Sunday.

A vast, modern Exhibition Palace, known as **Palexpo** (7981111), adjoining Geneva's Cointrin Airport, was opened in 1981 and enlarged a few years later. It is now used for trade shows and conventions. The International Motor Show (Salon d'Auto) in March is outstanding.

Near Palexpo is the cubic, modern building of the World Trade Center (7989989) with facilities for visiting business executives and offices of the Geneva Chamber of Commerce and Industry.

SIDE TRIPS

Mont-Salève, although only 6 miles (10 kilometers) south of Geneva's center, is already in France; it is nevertheless a favorite weekend destination of many Genevans. Budding alpinists practice on its rocks, hang-gliding enthusiasts take off from its cliffs, and hikers walk along its ridge. The panorama from the 4,287-feet (1,307-meter) mountain embraces the lake, the city of Geneva, and the Rhône Valley.

Take the No. 8 bus from the Rond-Point de Rive, near the eastern end of the Rue du Rhône, to the Swiss border at the village of Veyrier (last stop at Veyrier-Douane, the customs control point). On French territory, beyond the railroad line, is the terminal of a cable-car system that takes passengers up to 3,600 feet (1,098 meters) altitude. A restaurant with a fine view is near the upper cable-car terminal. Intrepid tourists climb the Mont-Salève on the former roadbed of a disused railway starting near the lower cable-car terminal. For those who ride the cable car both ways, a trip to the Mont-Salève belvedere from the center of Geneva and back needn't take more than three hours.

Another pleasant outing is the **Cruise of Famous Residences.** This lake cruise is offered by competing organizations whose boats all depart from Quai du Mont-Blanc (p. 155). Various versions of the trip range in duration from forty minutes to two hours and cost from $6 to $15 (half price for children between the ages of four and twelve; children under four travel free). Commentaries in French, English, and other languages over the public address system point out the sights ashore.

Shortly after departure passengers see the Palais Wilson, the Villa Bartholoni, and the Botanical Garden and United Nations complex. (See pp. 182–84.)

Other notable buildings on the north shore include the Villa de l'Impératrice, where Napoléon's first wife, Josephine Beauharnais, spent almost a year in exile, 1810–11, after the French emperor had annulled their marriage and demoted her from empress to a mere duchess of Navarre. Curiously, Napoléon's second wife, Marie Louise of Austria, also lived in the villa on two occasions, in 1820 and 1829.

Farther northeast are a chateau belonging to the Rothschild family, and the Maison de Saussure, an early-eighteenth-century villa in a park. The latter property is named after the Geneva physician and geologist Horace-Bénédict de Saussure (1740–99), who wrote about his travels in the Alps. (He was the first mountain climber to conquer Mont Blanc.) President Eisenhower resided in the villa in 1955.

After the Villa Barakat, one of the residences of the Aga Khan's family, the towered castle of the old village of Coppet comes into sight. The historic stronghold, dating from the thirteenth century and recently rebuilt, was once owned by the Geneva banker Jacques Necker (1732–1804), who served as France's finance minister under King Louis XVI. His daughter, the famous Madame de Staël (née Germaine Necker), wrote her most important works in the chateau between 1805 and 1817 and received there such contemporary celebrities as Lord Byron and François-Auguste-René de Chateaubriand.

At this point the cruise boat veers and sails into French waters. Near the French–Swiss border is a chalet in which Lenin and his wife lived for some time. A medieval hilltop tower, a remnant of a former castle, overlooks the first Swiss village on the south shore, Hermance.

As the boat proceeds toward Geneva, the seventeenth-century castle of Bellerive becomes visible. Next is the Villa Diodati on the hillside in the Genevan suburb of Cologny, a country house once owned by the family of Jean Diodati, an early-seventeenth-century leader of the Protestant Reformation movement in Geneva. The most famous tenant of the villa was Byron in the summer of 1816, after he had separated from his wife. He did plenty of writing there while continuing an affair with Jane ("Claire") Clairmont, half sister of Mary Wollstonecraft Godwin, who just had eloped from England with Percy Bysshe Shelley.

Mary, who was soon to become Mrs. Shelley, wrote much of *Frankenstein or The Modern Prometheus*, the horror classic, at Cologny, using a romanticized Mont-Salève as backdrop. Shelley and the two half sisters who were accompanying him lived that summer in a house near the Villa Diodati; they saw Byron almost daily.

From Cologny the cruise boat returns to its starting point coasting along the Parc des Eaux-Vives.

The Lake Geneva shipping companies, the official Geneva Tourist Office, and Key Tours, 7 Rue des Alpes (7314140), a commercial organization backed by international and Swiss travel services, suggest many other individual and group tour packages to places around Lake Geneva, the Rhône Valley, and other destinations in Switzerland, France, and Italy.

Index